Walking on Water

An Entrepreneurs Guidebook

TYLER NASSAU

SAN-920-0428

ISBN-10: 0615522076

ISBN-978-0-615-52207-4

The Library of Congress Cataloguing-in-Publication data is on file.
Printed in the United States of America
First Printing: July 1, 2013
Trademarks

"The distance between genius and insanity is measured only by success."

ELLIOT CARVER - JAMES BOND VILLAIN

*This book is dedicated to the people who
inspired me to be who I am today:*

*My parents, Bernd and Veronika,
Sir Richard Branson, and Anthony Robbins*

Table of Contents

Introduction

When I started my renewable energy business a couple of years ago, I was told by people that once I secured a power purchase agreement from a utility I would be able to easily access money to grow my business. Not so. When I secured the agreement, I was told that if I built the wind farm, money would come. Wrong again. When I built it, I was told there would be even more money when I took the company public. Didn't happen. I felt like I was on a treadmill trying to reach that ever-elusive pot of fame and fortune, only to realize that I had built a multi-million dollar business that survives to this day, long after I sold it.

We hear about Google and Microsoft, and all the instant Facebook billionaires, but in fact, most entrepreneurs end up having to make our money the normal way —by trial and error—without the benefit of being in the limelight of fame. There are also many who fail, even before they ever get a chance to prove themselves. And unlike many other successful entrepreneurs, I make no excuses about my ups and downs and the trials and tribulations of starting a business. But I have also started more than just one. To date I have incorporated about twenty-seven companies. One was an absolute disaster and had to be shut down, fifteen were running OK but didn't make it big, and five were extremely successful. Of those last five companies, I sold four and took one public. If you put it into context, that puts my rate of failure for a business startup at about 60 percent, not bad considering the national average is 98 percent. However, I'd like to think of it more as a 40 percent success rate instead of being 2 percent for the national average. I have also raised about $177 million in venture and working capital over the years, with my last company achieving a year-over-year revenue growth of about 700 percent. The most important statistic, however, is that I only lost about $40,000 on the one failed business without losing a single penny of investor capital.

So there are two things I would like you to glean from the numbers above: one, my rate of success for new businesses is above the national average and two, I didn't lose a lot of money on the business I shut down.

Over the last eighteen years of being an entrepreneur, I have come up with a formula for creating pretty much any business in any country and any industry. At first I thought I had a personal skill that set me apart from others, but my success created a lot of ripples on Facebook with friends and family. They saw a massive change in my lifestyle, going from pretty much bread and water to private jets, yachts, and St. Barth's vacations. And after attending a couple of Business Mastery events with Tony Robbins in Fiji, people started asking me questions as to how they could improve their own businesses. I wasn't even a speaker at the event. I was just trying to get out of the office, have an excuse to go to Fiji, and have a legitimate reason to write it off, so to speak.

At first I shrugged off this newfound interest, but when I started helping my friends, family members, and even high school buddies in places as far away as Germany, Sweden, and Australia, I realized that this formula worked for anyone. I then decided to help some random people that I had met in Fiji, and last I checked, a couple of them just took their companies public. Come to think of it, I should have charged them something for my services as a consultant, but I wasn't in it for the money. I just knew I was on to something. I also knew that because my own businesses operated in multiple countries and continents, I was pretty comfortable that this is a global formula that works just about anywhere.

Ultimately, you need to get yourself organized when you are starting a new venture. That means that you cannot simply rely on a great idea and wait for a high net worth individual to give you money based on that idea, and then make instant profits or wait for that ever distant sale of the business. More importantly, you need to set your own milestones, reach them, and ultimately create the success on your own, and only then will money follow. Don't rely on that future pot of gold, but rather, ensure that you have daily cash flow to survive and thrive personally. This book is intended to give you an outline of what you need to do in order to get yourself to that point. It is a brief insight into my formula of steps I've taken that I believe will work for any startup.

But just so you know a little more about me, I figured I'd give you a bit of my history. My family has been in the energy business for over 120 years, starting in 1892 when my great-great grandfather decided to convert some of his old flour mills into run of the river hydro-generation facilities. That was about eight years after Thomas Edison invented the light bulb. Subsequently, my grandfather and then my father ran that business for over one hundred years. So, I come from a long line of successful entrepreneurs. Being self-employed is in my DNA, but it also means I have very large shoes to fill. In 1985, my father decided to sell our company to EnBW AG, in turn creating the third largest utility in the country, which has now grown to over six million customers and energy revenues exceeding □18 Billion (2010). In 1985, we immigrated to Canada. I was about nine years old at the time. My father decided to get into the hotel and restaurant business (a lifelong dream of his) and was involved in many new hotel developments such as Delta Hotels and Journey's End (now Comfort Inn and Quality Inn), and he launched a successful restaurant in the greater Toronto area together with my mother.

After a couple of years, my parents decided they wanted to take over a couple of hotels in the outskirts of Munich, Bavaria. When I was eighteen, I decided that I would go to Montréal to study finance and international business at McGill University. Like any child who comes from a relatively rich family, I was a little spoiled. I took so much advantage of it that when I was around nineteen years old, my father decided to cut me off financially—and I mean completely. That's when I realized the value of the dollar. In about twenty-four hours, I went from spoiled rich kid to broke and hungry, particularly when I started to have mounting credit card debt and creditors began calling. There was a short period when I was collecting pennies and quarters to ensure I had enough money to buy some small fries at McDonald's for my day's meal. So I learned the hard way. There were a lot of hard feelings against my dad, initially, which over the years turned into respect and gratitude, because I never would have risen to such heights on my own if I had not gone through those hardships.

I finally understood the stories my grandfather told me about losing everything. He had lost everything to the Nazis in the Second World War when all of our copper power lines and electricity generators in the Black Forest were confiscated from our power plants. Having spent the war years in exile in France, my grandfather and his wife were left with nothing at the end of the war, except some suitcases with personal belongings and crumbling homes and buildings that had been mostly destroyed. But that didn't stop my grandfather and his brother from going back, picking up the pieces and starting anew. It was not only for their sake, but because they were delivering a much needed commodity—electricity. The people in post-war Germany and France needed us.

It was at that point, when I had lost everything and was no different from any other bum on the street, I learned my lesson—I had to apply an iron will to ensure that I was financially independent, no matter what life threw at me. So I went about starting new businesses. And to avoid writing an entire book in this introduction, I am going to give you a quick excerpt of some of the most noteworthy ones.

As my first attempt at business, I decided to start a record label that focused on importing records from Europe, mostly electronic and dance music. When a hit would come out in Europe, I would try to license it for all of North America; then when the big record labels in the United States finally realized it was a hit, they would have to come to talk to me. That business went OK, but I got myself into hot water when I decided to start developing my own artists. I spent hundreds of thousands of dollars developing local Canadian artists, only for them to sell less than stellar amounts of records. I needed to find a new medium.

Montréal was not really a good city for business, which led me to move to Toronto. While there, I started getting into the online media game, building some of the largest Internet websites of the time. This was during the dot.com boom and the days of MP3.com—when the recording industry was still unaware of their future demise. Some of my bands started making hundreds of thousands of dollars on the Internet by having their music downloaded and tied in with advertising. I was finally on top of my game when at this point the Recording Industry Association of America decided to sue everyone off the Internet. When I was told to destroy one year of my work and take everything down, I said, "You guys don't know your business model anymore." That's when I left the music business for good and ended up founding another company called Line

Entertainment Holdings Inc. together with my long-term business partner Wayne.

Line Entertainment was an advertising, marketing, and television production company. We focused on product launches and street marketing campaigns. Some of our clients included the Virgin Group of companies such as Virgin Mobile and Virgin Atlantic, Louis Vuitton, Moet Hennessy, Twentieth Century Fox Film Corporation, Twentieth Century Fox Home Video, and CBC radio. The Virgin gig also gave me access to one of the most successful billionaire entrepreneurs in the world, a connection that would later grow to a mutual respect and co-operation on charitable initiatives. Nothing like being able to send an email to Sir Richard Branson when you have a business question. Sometime in 2002, my business partner Wayne and I noticed an opportunity in the digital television space. With all these new digital channels on the cable networks, we quickly realized they were desperate for content. Not knowing anything about the TV business, we decided to create a couple of pilot TV shows including a travel show and a cooking show. Recognizing the importance of timing for market entry, we were one of the fastest growing media companies in the early 2000s.

During my media days, I had continued to invest some of my personal money into wind projects in Germany, never letting go of my family's roots in the renewable energy business. So in September of 2003, when the lights went out across the northeastern seaboard of the US and Canada and our politicians started to de-regulate the electricity market, I decided to re-launch the family business, this time as a Canadian company. With about six months of prep work, I finally incorporated the business on April 16, 2004. For the first time in the history of all my business startups, my father actually thought this was a good idea. The day I put my father on my company's payroll was the day when I felt like I had achieved the ultimate success. I was further rewarded by being able to bury the hatchet, tap his expertise, and create probably one of the most rewarding experiences in my life—working with my dad.

Over the next three years my team and I built a 2.2 billion dollar portfolio of about 3,000 MW of wind and solar development projects in the United States, Canada, and the Caribbean, starting with two simple wind turbines called The Providence Bay Wind Farm on Manitoulin Island. Similar to a real estate developer, our goal was to develop and permit projects and then sell them on to the large utilities and investment funds, making a handsome 250 percent return on our investment each time we flipped a project. I even went as far as helping my previous clients to design completely off-grid power solutions, including Richard Branson and his team, where I assisted in designing a wind and solar system for his private island in the British Virgin Islands. Our company's revenue growth was exceeding 700 percent per annum, but I soon realized that we would need to access more capital and that could only be done south of the border.

In 2008, I took the company public on the Toronto Venture Exchange with all the fanfare, hoopla, securities filings, and fireworks of that process. My personal net worth skyrocketed from zero to millions in 4.6 seconds of hitting the button to open the markets. That was a rush to say the least, the most venerable day in my life. My timing was immaculate, because I saw the doom of the recession looming right ahead of us. These insights came from my new board of directors, who warned me that this recession would be a monster. Just before the entire financial market locked up in September of that year, I managed to raise sufficient capital for my company to weather the financial storm. With the volatile markets wreaking havoc on stock portfolios, my net worth was fluctuating by a million dollars on a daily basis, so I got into the habit of not looking at the stock price. But the company had money to grow, and I had an excellent income and job security because I was the boss—not a bad position to be in going into the worst economic recession of a generation.

At the height of the credit crisis, I knew that as a developer we would continue to be at the mercy of the economy's cyclicality, and so I began looking for ways to diversify the company into other renewable technology related businesses. A key characteristic of any good management team is the ability to see what is coming down the road. Seeing the credit crisis continuing through 2012 and wanting to ensure our company's long-term survival whilst diversifying my portfolio, we bet the company on a single M & A transaction (mergers and acquisitions).

In April 2010, I sold my Company to a NASDAQ listed U.S. multinational for about US$20 million, further bolstering our business and in turn becoming one of its largest shareholders. In hindsight, that gutsy move is what allowed us to survive the great recession. Six of our nearest competitors ended up going out of business—and because we had access to capital, it allowed us to buy their assets out of bankruptcy.

Today, the combined Company remains one of America's leading renewable technology companies. And although I sold out and moved on, the company to this day is still around and active in areas including hybrid power-train systems, solar module manufacturing, renewable energy, lightweight gaseous storage systems, and defense contracting—with an overall goal of emissions reduction in all areas of our daily lives. Even though assets may have changed hands, I can still drive by the wind farms and say "I built that". That's something to be proud of, and not a bad legacy to leave behind either.

Since then I have moved on to better and greater things. My passion has never been running a business, but starting new businesses. It's where I thrive, it's what I know, and it's where the most money can be made. I'm passionate about starting companies.

And now it is your turn...

CHAPTER I

The Beginning

I Have an Idea—Now What?

That's great! Every single great company has sprung from an original idea by one person. But do not think for a minute that you are the only one with this idea. The sheer fact that there are seven billion people on this planet means that at any given point in time there will be another one hundred people with the same idea. What sets you apart from the rest is your ability to raise money, to follow through on your idea to make it a reality, and the skills to stand out from the crowd. It boils down to motivation, perseverance, tactics, and a bit of humility every now and then.

There are four reasons why 98 percent of all new businesses fail within the first five years:

1. Your timing is off
2. You are underfinanced
3. You have the wrong team
4. You didn't do your homework

Fortunately for you, you just bought this book (or perhaps you are reading it on your iPad as an e-book) which is designed to convey not only my words of wisdom, but also provide examples, downloads, and reference material that you can use (free of charge) to get organized, raise money, and get you on your way to success. The goal is that by the time you have finished reading this book you will have some key tools and the knowledge you need to make your mark as an entrepreneur. And hopefully, if applied right, the house advantage might just be in your favour.

Your timing is off

No matter how good your product is, and no matter how much money you raise initially, if your timing is off, you will fail. If there's one thing you should have gleaned from the introduction of this book, it is that every time I started something new, it was in response to some market disruption event—the rise of mp3s and digital TV, and a power blackout. A good example of this is PayPal. You see, PayPal didn't start out as the world's leading online payment system. In fact, the company floundered at first as a device-to-device payment system for Palm Pilots. At that time, the concept of a smartphone, iPhone, iPad and a mobile payment solution for all of these was foreign to consumers. They didn't even have debit card payments in those days. Almost bankrupt and out of money,

PayPal, with the invention of the web browser, finally realized the potential of online payment systems for websites. This market shift allowed PayPal to become the success it is today. And it is only now, almost ten years later, that device payment solutions are realistic because the market and consumer mindset have both caught up to the technology. I'm sure by this point someone has dusted off that old business plan from the 1990s.

You are underfinanced

When you start a new business, you will never be an expert until you have paid your dues and spent a couple of years running a company. So it is nearly impossible for an entrepreneur to know exactly how much money he or she will need to stage and launch a business. You can make an educated guess. But ask any successful entrepreneur, and he will tell you that whatever number you come up with, triple it. So if your budget is $50,000, you will most likely need $150,000. If you think you need $10 million, you probably need $30 million. It's that simple. Now you can probably see why, even if you have $50,000 to start your business, you could run into trouble very fast—because you have no cushion to weather unexpected events. In later chapters, we will determine exactly how and what you need, and for which things you should use personal funds versus investor funds. I will also introduce you to what I call the 10 million dollar formula.

You have the wrong team

The interplay of you and the people who work with you can either make or break your business. I am not just talking about employees, but professionals, lawyers, and advisors. Companies have risen and fallen depending on who the founders have surrounded themselves with. There are a lot of terrible preconceived notions in venture capital circles. Not many people talk about it, but the bias is out there. Legendary investor John Doerr made a telling, offhand remark a few years ago at a venture capital conference. He observed that the "world's greatest entrepreneurs" are almost all "white male nerds who've dropped out of Harvard or Stanford." That really rubs me the wrong way, because my experience tells me that anyone, no matter what his or her background, race, religion, sexual orientation or even education can have a successful business. You just need to know your personal shortcomings and augment them with a great team. With the right combination, you will not only shine in the eyes of the market, but you will reduce your business risk by ensuring a higher chance of success. We are going to spend a considerable amount of time on this subject later in the book, because it is vital to understand who fits with you and your personality. What you need is your Dream Team.

You didn't do your homework

This is one area where some of the biggest mistakes happen. Many founders jump at the chance of opening a new business, spending lavish amounts on new office space, retail decorations, signs, branding, and business cards—but not a single penny (or time) is spent on research. People are willing to believe their own convictions without actually considering the market forces at play, the real profit margins, the barriers to entry, and worst of all, they underestimate their competitors. This is probably one of the fastest ways to go bankrupt. I have spent hundreds of thousands of dollars on businesses that I have walked away from because I found a fatal flaw in the business model. We will delve into the details of what I do to identify these issues before you ever spend a single dollar on the business.

Who Are You?

The Ancient Greek aphorism "Know thyself" was inscribed in the forecourt of the Temple of Apollo at Delphi. What is true in ancient times is true today, particularly in business, because if you know yourself, you have already won half the battle. So, who are you? You might identify yourself with the word *entrepreneur*, but what type of entrepreneur are you? Maybe you are a skilled and talented producer of something that meets the needs of a particular marketplace. Perhaps you are good at leading and managing people. Furthermore, you might be able to tolerate risk and have a knack for identifying opportunities. Maybe you are a combination of all these attributes. What is important is to understand who you are so that the team you choose matches your traits, augments your talents, and is proficient in the skills you may be lacking.

In business, there are three types of distinct entrepreneurial personalities:

Artist/Talent—This is someone of extraordinary talent who consistently meets the needs of a marketplace.

Manager/Leader—This is someone who consistently and effectively manages and meets the needs of an artist so that he or she can consistently meet the needs of the market. Even though these people have management skills, they don't necessarily have leadership skills.

Visionary—This person is the creator and holder of the vision, the person who attracts and effectively engages managers/leaders. A visionary entrepreneur has a high level of risk tolerance and is able to personally weather the economic and emotional ups and downs of the business. This person is willing to take on significant risk. Visionary entrepreneurs work with managers to create and build a business system that consistently empowers skilled producers and talented artists to meet the needs of the market they serve.

You might say that you have some or all of these traits, but there will always be one that stands out; this will be the one you lean toward the most. To figure out which one you are, ask yourself the following five questions:

1. Who am I?
2. What are my talents?
3. What do I truly love most?
4. What do I like doing the least?
5. Who else do I need to help me optimize my business results?

You might be starting out on your own, but there will come a time in the life of your company when you can no longer do everything. That means you will need to hire people to keep the business functioning and thriving from day to day. By answering the five questions to determine your strengths and weaknesses, you can also determine the type of person you need on your team to help you thrive and be a success.

How to Get Started

When starting a business, the first two things that come to mind are "How do I register a business?" and secondly, "How do I go about opening a business bank account?"

To answer the first question, find the website for your state, and then do a search for the department that oversees corporations. You will find instructions for how to form various types of companies, but the most common are corporations, limited partnerships, and sole proprietorships. Rather than providing you the pros and cons of each of these business structures, I will make it very simple for you. You are in the game of success, and you are looking to raise money. There is only one type of company that you should form, and that is a corporation, also known as C corporation (not an S corporation). There are three reasons to incorporate your business:

1. You should always keep your business separate from your personal life, particularly when it comes to finances. You have to be under the assumption that you're going to get audited by the government or the IRS. There is nothing worse than having a government auditor searching through your personal bank account statement on a quarterly basis and you needing to clarify private and personal expenditures.

2. A C corporation provides you some protection when it comes to liability. In this day and age, particularly in America, there are more lawyers than entrepreneurs, and chances are even if you become successful, someone will want to sue you at some point in time. A corporation is great because it limits the liability of the individual shareholder to the original investment. Now that doesn't mean somebody can't sue you, but it certainly is a better situation than if you were a sole proprietor with all your personal assets at stake.

3. Thirdly, and most importantly, by having a corporation, you can borrow from the bank, and you can seek out potential investors that might want to invest in your business. You can issue partial ownership (shares), which gives you a certain amount of prestige with clients.

Let's tackle the next question. Where do you incorporate? In the United States, there are multiple options for incorporating your business. In fact, you can incorporate in pretty much any state. Each individual state government has its own office or Secretary of State to which you apply to incorporate your business. There are fees, and some states' fees are higher than others. Generally, the best state in which to incorporate a company is the state of Delaware, which can be done even if you don't reside in that state. Delaware has the most companies registered in America, and because of this, it has the most case law in relation to business disputes. More case law means more protection for you. There are two exceptions to this rule. If you incorporate in the state of Delaware, but you are doing business, for example, in New York, you will need to apply for a state license to operate your business. New York is notorious for expensive licenses and it can be costly to pay a fee in both Delaware and in New York. If money is a concern, incorporate within your state. Some states offer a license fee exemption if you meet certain small business requirements.

It is also best not to incorporate in Delaware if you are located in a zero state income tax locale such as Nevada. In Nevada, it makes more sense to incorporate there if your business will be located there to save taxes and avoid the $500 annual license fee that out-of-state corporations must pay to do business in that state. In fact, if you incorporate locally you can qualify for the business license fee exemption for small businesses.

To summarize, you are going to form a C corporation in the state of Delaware, and you are going to get a business license in the individual state in which you plan to business. Once you have your incorporation documents and state license, you will need to apply for an Employer Identification Number (also known as an EIN). It is essentially a tax ID number that helps the Federal government (the IRS) identify your company. You can obtain an EIN by following this link: www.irs.gov.

With these three items in hand, you are now ready to open your corporate bank account. Most banks will require that you bring all this paperwork with you to open a business checking account. Once you have done so, you will have successfully separated your personal finances from your business finances.

Following these steps can be a daunting task. I suggest you use a company such as the Delaware Company (www.thedelawarecompany.com) or Biz Filings (www.bizfilings.com) as your one-stop shop to get it all done, inexpensively and fast. The nice thing about them is that not only will they help you search for, register, and secure your business name, but more importantly, they will also help you with the incorporation process and the individual state licensing and respective tax accounts that you will need to open up with the IRS and the state government. All the required documents will be FedExed to you in a couple of days. As your registered agent, they will monitor everything over the years to make sure you remain in compliance, file your taxes on time, and renew your licences annually.

If you are reading this book outside of the United States, there are equivalent companies in Canada, the United Kingdom, and pretty much anywhere in continental Europe that will help you become incorporated. There are even such companies in offshore areas such as the Caribbean, Gibraltar, the Cayman Islands, and Malta. It just might take a bit longer to search for them. Here is a list of my favourite international legal service providers, and I know they are reputable with excellent customer service:

Norton Rose Fullbright – Canada/USA/UK

CSB Group – Malta (European Union)

Appleby – BVI, London, Hong Kong, Shanghai, Zurich

Higgs & Johnson – Bahamas

Morgan & Morgan – Republic of Panama

By the way, at this stage, don't worry so much about choosing the perfect company name. We will tackle the subject of branding and marketing in a later chapter.

CHAPTER 2

Planning And Goal Setting

The Long Road to Success

My father once said to me, "Your life will never turn out how you plan it." At first, I ignored that word of wisdom, but I soon realized that it applies to pretty much all areas, including your plans for your new business venture. When I was young, I set myself a goal of becoming a millionaire by age twenty-one. What people forgot to tell me was that I had to start three mediocre businesses to get to the diamond. It took me until I was thirty to hit the mark—but then I made up for it by becoming a multi-millionaire. Of course, by the time I was twenty-five I was feeling somewhat frustrated by my efforts until I watched a biography about Dave Thomas, the founder of Wendy's. I took comfort in the fact that he was only thirty when he made his first million—and that was before he started Wendy's. He made his first million with three Kentucky Fried Chicken franchises, a little known fact about the man who had Colonel Sanders as a mentor.

Unless you have a Microsoft or Google idea that is started in a garage, the average entrepreneur will no doubt have to start a couple of times to get it right, but that's OK. Statistics will tell you that starting a company like Google is like winning the lottery—it's nearly impossible. So the rest of us will just have to make money with companies that most Americans will probably never hear of. But for all of this uncertainty, it's good to have a road map of where you want to be and how you are going to get there: your business plan.

When I think of a business plan, my mind conjures up an image of a massive dusty binder filled with useless words that nobody will ever read. If that image comes to your mind, too, forget about those old notions of a business plan; they have become obsolete in the twenty-first century. Now you are probably wondering why a book on starting a business would tell you to bypass the business plan, right? Good. My goals is to delete what they taught you in school or worse, in university, and to teach you what people actually use in the real world to run a successful business.

Reinventing the Business Plan

Most successful entrepreneurs will tell you stories about how their companies were started from ideas scrawled on the back of a cocktail napkin. Most professionals, bankers, and accountants will tell you it is important to write a hundred-page detailed business plan. So which is it? Three things to remember:

1. You don't have time to write a book.
2. Your plan will be outdated within two weeks of your first investor meetings.
3. You need to know your business plan by heart anyway.

I think a lot of one's success has to do with flexibility. You see, the reason why the cocktail napkin business plan is successful is because its small size allows room for you to just state a goal and nothing else, which leaves you with immense flexibility to reach that goal, whereas the banker's business plan is chock full of details, data, and ways to get there with a well-researched background. Unfortunately, neither will get you money from investors. The napkin plan doesn't show that you know your stuff, and the banker's plan is too rigid and boring. Nobody reads it. I wrote a business plan once; I don't think I ever read it myself.

Very early in my career as an entrepreneur, I learned that investors want to get an understanding of your business without having to read a book. This really stems from the fact that they are considering several business opportunities per day, and there is simply not enough time for them to wade through a lengthy business plan. Over the years, I have found a happy medium that has worked repeatedly. I call it the Ten Million Dollar Formula. That's because I have never raised less than ten million dollars using it. It is comprised of three key items:

1. A two-page executive summary
2. A power point presentation of no more than ten to twelve slides
3. A term sheet

All three combined is what I call your Staging Kit. Each of these items serves a specific purpose. The executive summary is used as **bait** to get the meeting, the power point presentation is for the **song and dance,** and the term sheet is for the **slam dunk.** If you are somewhat perplexed by this terminology, rest assured that by the end of this chapter you will know exactly what these terms mean.

A little warning: Walking around with presentations and term sheets is frowned upon by the SEC. That is because securities law says you can't just go door-to-door offering shares in your company to any random potential investor. More important for you, it could get you into trouble because your presentation and term sheet could be construed as an offering document that is assumed to disclose any and all risks to the investor, which is impossible to do unless you file an IPO document (initial public offering). In short, you could get sued if what you put in there turns out to be inaccurate, or worse, you miss your milestones. Always, always, always seek legal counsel that specializes in corporate finance before you attempt to raise money for your business (see my later chapter about lawyers).

The Bait—Your Executive Summary

The executive summary is something that you can send in an email to a potential investor without looking desperate. What I mean by that is the investor will want to make up his mind whether he is interested well before he meets you or before you drown him in due diligence material. But a power point presentation sometimes lacks the ability to convey the essence or finer details of your business—which should be reserved for an in-person meeting.

The nice thing about a two-page limit is that it forces you to condense all of your ideas, ambitions, milestones, and financing requirements. There is no room to ramble. As you are writing and condensing your executive summary, having the two-page limit in mind will force you to throw things out that are not necessarily important—and if they are not important to the investor or your pitch, chances are your business doesn't need them anyway. Use the K.I.S.S. principle—**K**eep **I**t **S**imple **S**tupid. The details are for you to know—potential investors are only interested in the big-picture view, such as what makes your business unique in your intended market. Don't get technical unless the investor asks detailed questions, or if the investor you are meeting is an expert in your field.

The executive summary serves only one purpose: to get you a meeting and to weed out the people who will waste your time. There is nothing worse than pitching an investor who isn't keenly interested in your industry or idea.

The Song and Dance—Your Power Point Presentation

The term "song and dance" actually comes from the advertising industry, a group of people that gives presentations every day to potential brand name clients that are willing to fork over millions to ad agencies. But if you think about it, that's exactly what your presentation is. You have but a mere minute to impress your audience. Think of Paul Potts or Susan Boyle on the stage of Britain's Got Talent—everybody laughed at them until they opened their mouths and sang.

Your power point presentation should not be longer than twelve slides, including a Forward Looking Statements disclaimer that your attorney can prepare for you on the second slide, and your address on the last slide. That gives you precisely ten slides to make your point.

There is a specific format to follow for building a successful slide presentation. Since this format is somewhat of an industry norm with investment bankers, you need to know it. I have seen millionaires giving new business presentations only to lose the entire audience on the third slide, mainly because they didn't follow the standard sequence.

The standard format your presentation should maintain is as follows:

1. **Title** – a slide with your Company logo and slogan
2. **Cautionary Note** – a legal disclaimer regarding Forward Looking Statements
3. **Investment Opportunity** – a quick summary of how much you are looking for and what it will achieve for the Company and the investor
4. **Business Model** – a quick overview of what sets you apart from the rest (think niche, old vs. new etc)
5. **Strategy** – indicate how you will get from A to B whilst creating revenue and net asset value.
6. **Product Overview** – Showcase your two best products with simple bullet points about how much you can sell, anything special about it and whether you have all the relevant permits/licenses.
7. **Strategic Relationships** – identify who your suppliers and partners are.
8. **Management Team** – Highlight using point form the three top employees that will make it all happen – showcase experience here. You should be one of them.
9. **Competitive Landscape** – In a graphic, show where you are in relation to your major competition.

10. **Investment Highlights** – Summarize your presentation – one point for each previous slide.
11. **Contact Info** – a slide with your name and contact information

The Slam Dunk—Your Term Sheet

A term sheet is a piece of paper with a table that simply outlines the terms of your contemplated money-raising efforts. It includes items such as how much you are seeking, use of proceeds, shares outstanding, and the price you are willing to sell a share in your business. This is something you keep on the side to be distributed after your presentation, once you have established there is keen interest in your proposition.

TIP: *Make sure your presentation matches the term sheet and the executive summary. You wouldn't believe how frustrated some investor types get if the numbers don't match! They see it as carelessness, even if it was just an honest mistake.*

CHAPTER 3

Act As If

The Look of Success

Unlike most stories of starting your business in your shabbiest pair of underwear, let's get real. The hippie look of startups and their dot.com ultra casual founders only works for people with at least seven zeros on their bank balance. If you already have a business that is producing mega cash flows, then by all means, wear flip-flops. But chances are that if you are reading this book, you don't. Most of the people who will give you money are still from the old suit-and-tie guard. And you will never see them without either unless they are in bed or golfing. So that means you need to be their equal, at least in terms of clothing. I might have been working out of my bachelor pad in my undies, but I made a point to buy myself one really good suit. It cost a fortune, somewhere around three thousand dollars. I ate Macaroni and Cheese out of a box for a month, but when I walked into that meeting room, I got instant respect, even if I was only twenty-two at the time. In later years, I started buying Brioni suits, and they still killed my wallet. Nine thousand dollars for one suit is still insane, even if I can afford it. But when I walk into a room these days, I garner instant attention as someone to be reckoned with. And you can always spot the guy in the cheap suit.

A good example: my fashion obsessed friend Scott decided to drag me to a Louis Vuitton store to buy something he didn't really need. The sales guy selling a thousand-dollar wallet was dressed in a two-for-one suit that probably cost him about $150. I thought to myself, *talk about having no leverage as a sales person.* If his employer really wanted to sell a high end product, he needs to look the part. How can you recommend or sell a product that is supposed to elevate your importance when the person selling it doesn't look like he is buying into the idea? If I'm a shopkeeper selling a high end product, I would ensure my employees are dressed the part. Upon mentioning that fact to my friend Scott, he elaborated on this point. Why do realtors drive expensive cars? It's because they want to look successful in the eyes of a potential client, and as their mobile office, it represents them. Follow this simple rule, then: If you are meeting lawyers, investors, and accountants, dress to impress. Look like you don't need money. If you are meeting with suppliers, dress down and look like you can't afford it—and you'll secure that discount.

A good suit should always be tailored, never just off the rack. Also, it's all about the fabric. If you buy a $100 buy two get one free suit, people can tell a mile away. Trust me. Buy one good classic suit, three nice shirts, and a couple of ties. That way you can change your look if you are meeting the same people over the course of several meetings. The best brands for suits are Canali, Brioni, Boss, and Donna Karan. The best brands for ties are Hermes and Louis Vuitton, and make sure they are 100 percent silk. Ladies, you generally dress better than your male counterparts, so this chapter is the best excuse you will ever have to go buy that perfect new power suit.

Now let's talk about the one thing that most people forget: the shoes. I have seen people in expensive suits only to look down at their feet and see them wearing a rag of a shoe, banged up and unpolished. I have reprimanded employees for wearing crappy shoes at key meetings. Unless you are an executive at Nike, show up at meetings wearing black leather dress shoes. Always make sure they are polished and shining. Yes, that means you should spend at least fifteen to twenty minutes in the morning polishing your shoes. That's how the army does it, and that's what a civilized successful gentleman/woman does. Polish your shoes, people.

If you are absolutely lost in the fashion department, hire a Certified Image Consultant who will show you which colors work for you. He or she will help you clean out your closet and will take you shopping for key items missing in your wardrobe. Lynda Jean, my personal image consultant, certainly changed my life. I was stuck in a fashion rut, and she managed to make me look like the successful person I am, and the compliments keep coming. You can check out her services at www.lyndajean.com

Your Office

As an entrepreneur, you are generally on your own in the beginning. When I started my first business, I was living in a tiny bachelor apartment that had a bed, a desk, a PC, and a telephone, but that didn't stop me from looking like a successful businessman to the outside world. I had arranged for a virtual office in one of the Class

A skyscrapers downtown. A virtual office is a shared space that allows you to have a true office environment in which to conduct business. It provides you with a prestigious address and a phone number, a secretary who answers your calls, and the ability to have meetings with potential clients in full-scale conference rooms. You can have the look that you need to attract investors, but at a pay-per-use cost. Nothing says success more than inviting a potential supplier or investor to the fiftieth floor of your local landmark high-rise building. Even if you don't work in a large city, you can research the availability of shared office environments and virtual offices online for your city or town.

TIP: *I have found Regus to be one of the best companies out there. I currently have five or six offices with them—I have lost track. Check them out at www.regus.com.*

Talking vs. Doing

One thing that sets apart successful entrepreneurs from the ones that fail is an innate ability to follow through on their goals. Many people dream about goals, but few turn them into reality. When they see others succeeding, they excuse it by saying that person is lucky. Being successful has nothing to do with luck, but rather the willpower, the tenacity, and the right tools to create your own luck. But you need to take it one step further, because the road you take to attaining your goals is in the changing landscape of business. That means you need to be flexible enough to amend or change your approach on the fly. To-do lists are good, but they do not give you a road map that shows a detour you can take if you are facing a road-block—or worse, gridlock. To-do lists are also somewhat negative, because they entail things you must do, and there is a difference between *having* to do something and *wanting* to do something.

Having to and wanting to ultimately mean pain or pleasure. Our brains haven't really evolved much from our ancestors when it comes to these two little motivators. Your brain works on pain and pleasure. You will seek out everything that gives you pleasure and avoid everything that causes pain. This explains why we procrastinate about doing certain things; most likely it is because we associate something negative with them. At the same time, there are occasions when we will move mountains just to be able to find some time to do something fun. The key is to find ways to associate pleasure with the things that will run your business more effectively.

When this concept is applied to entrepreneurship, it means that you need to find something you are passionate about, have an interest in, and that it is fun to do. If you hate getting up in the morning to work on your new business, you are not going to succeed. If you like going to work in the morning and enjoy every hour of growing your business, then your chances of success quadruple. The passion you have for your business will make you look successful, even when you're still growing and barely able to pay the bills. If there is stress, it is good stress, because you are generating it; it is not being forced on your by someone else. I could write a book about this concept and the motivational forces that go behind it, but there is a person much more qualified than I am to teach you this, and man is the über guru of motivation and self-improvement, Tony Robbins (www.tonyrobbins.com). Over the years I have successfully used some of his tools and techniques to get where I am today.

As I mentioned in the introduction, when my father cut me off financially, I was down and out and as broke as anyone could be. That year I was watching one of Tony Robbins's infomercials late at night. After watching the darn thing for about two hours, I was finally convinced to spend my last $299 dollars to buy his Personal Power II CD set. That was over fifteen years ago. I can say with all honesty that ever since I finished that program my life has been on fast forward. To meet the ever-changing demands of the business world, I needed a system that kept me motivated, could be amended on the fly, and ensured that I break down my major goals into easy-to-do daily steps. One thing that has helped me immensely in achieving this is the Rapid Planning Method (RPM) developed by Tony. It's an easy to use system, complete with a binder to keep track of your major goals while fitting them into your hectic daily schedule. While you're at it, throw in one of his Unleash the Power Within seminars—there's nothing better to get you motivated to launch your new company. In fact, I make it a habit to attend one of his seminars every couple of years to get myself back on track, or whenever I am launching a new business.

If you are the skeptical type, all I can say is to give it a try. If it works, great, if it doesn't, send it back and get your money refunded. RPM is a very valuable and valid tool in your arsenal to beat the competition and grow a successful business.

Shadowing and Mentoring

Three key people have influenced how I do business: Anthony Robbins, Sir Richard Branson, and Donald Trump. In fact, some people might say I have an obsession with modelling myself after these people. But it's not some weird fan obsession. Rather, it's so that I learn how to do things the right way the first time without making too many mistakes. These men are a source of inspiration and a measurement of my own success. These guys have a ten to twenty-year head start over me, so there is always something I can learn from them. There is more to it than that, though.

Modelling yourself after someone else can be an amazing catalyst to your own success. What does that mean? To make it real, here are the results it got for me. I successfully started a company that is now publicly listed on the NASDAQ. I own homes in places like Las Vegas and the Bahamas. I travel via private jet (whenever I can get over the guilt of wasting money and harming the environment). I even once bought a picturesque island off the shores of Nova Scotia. I commute between all of these places because I have extricated myself from the daily running of the business and can provide for my family and friends as I please. It's not because I'm a genius; it's simply because I based my decisions and actions on other people's successes and failures.

Every time I went against the advice of a mentor, my net worth suffered. Here is a good example. As I previously mentioned, I helped Sir Richard Branson's management team plan a renewable power system on Necker Island. One afternoon, after a morning spent hiking the hills with engineers, I was sitting in the pool by the beach on Necker Island together with Sir Richard when, with a twinkle in my eyes, I announced that I was going to take my company public. By way of reply, I was given a thirty-minute story by Sir Richard of his own negative experiences in the process of going public. Three years later, I must confess, I should have listened to him. Could I have avoided three years of terror and $2 million in personal losses? Sure. Was I arrogant to think I could do it better than the master of all startups? Totally. Lesson learned? Yes—painfully. But do not worry. If going public is your dream, I have devoted an entire chapter to the process and the pitfalls so that you can do it and get out while you can…and fast. Or, you can sell the business—that's what I do most of the time.

The Importance of Gray Hair

Investors invest in you and your accomplishments more than they invest in your new product or idea. That is simply because experience tells them that someone who has done it before is much more likely to succeed again. If you are a first time entrepreneur, this is a very difficult catch-22 to overcome. This is where a board of advisors or directors comes into play. There is however a key difference between advisors and a board. Advisors advise, while directors can meddle in the affairs of your business. If you land a large investor, he or she will most likely want a seat on your board of directors, and that is something you need to consider very carefully. I have said no to people when I didn't think they would be in a position to make decisions in my best interests.

Consider also that some people might be hesitant to join the board of a startup company, so the concept of a board of advisors is valuable. But make sure it's not Uncle Bob and Aunt Helga. Preferably, the people on your board should be leaders in your industry. This is easier said than done, but make some effort here. Perhaps there is a consultant you are using who might want to advise (outside of his/her role as a billing professional). Good types of people to have on your board of advisors include accountants, lawyers, marketing people, and corporate financial professionals—the kind of people who can truly help your business or answer questions that will benefit your business. I was lucky in this regard. In my line of business, I have to use a lot of consultants, so I was able to get people from GE, Amec, and Deloitte & Touche on my board of advisors. When you throw around brand names like that, something curious happens. You become credible in the eyes of competitors, investors, and suppliers. Always ask to be able to use their names, then publish those on your website to give people confidence in your business. At the same time, you will hopefully gain some excellent free advice along the way.

Once you have raised your first round of capital you will inevitably end up having strangers join your board of directors. The longer you can delay that happening, the more freedom you will have to develop your business without interruption or meddling. Going public was a daunting task, made even more stressful because some overzealous board member decided to start an investigation into a decision I had made in error the second year after I started my business. That cost my company a quarter of a million dollars in fees to accountants, and I still haven't psychologically recovered from the stress. In the end, nothing happened. I remained president, the company was sold, and the disclosure of the event was brushed over by the purchaser as "growing pains." But I was seriously pissed off enough that for a period of three months I wanted to quit my own business. It's not a good thing when the founder of the business is pissed off and not wanting to do any work for the company he founded. My tip is, get your investment angels on the board, and always make sure the power of the board balances in your favor. For instance, if you run a private company and have five board members, make sure that at least three will side with you. If you go public, that will be more difficult to do because the process requires independent directors. But there will always be friends and foes. Make sure you become an expert at playing the game of political chess.

CHAPTER 4

Financing Your Business

Where Do I Find Money?

Let's face it. You are not Mark Zuckerberg of Facebook fame. So to expect leading venture capital firms such as Palo Alto Investors or Kleiner Perkins to be knocking at your door is completely unreasonable. More so, before these guys come along, you will most likely already have raised some startup capital. Rather than contemplating the various stages of venture capital, let's examine real and practical sources of funding for your new venture.

I believe there are four phases to any business: the *idea stage*, the *launch phase*, the *transition*, and the *exit*. For now, we will talk about the first two, as they are most relevant to you.

The Idea Stage

When you are in the early stages of forming a business, the idea stage, you are still forming your idea and figuring out your budgets and pro-forma, which is a five year financial forecast of revenues and profit. Nothing is certain yet, but you have an idea and you want to run with it. There are four sources of capital that you can tap: your savings account, your credit cards, your friends and family members, and your local bank. The amounts you are looking for will generally be in the low thousands, just enough to cover your initial company formation expenses, including incorporation, opening a bank account, registering a website and domain name, legal work, business cards, and setting up a small home (or virtual) office with a phone, fax, and PC. The dollar amounts should be small enough that if they are lost forever you can recover easily from the financial loss. Using your own money for these types of expenses can create an immense amount of value for very little investment. The reason I call this a stage is because that's what it is, similar to a real estate agent staging a house for sale, or a movie studio setting up a sound stage. It looks great from the front, but there are two-by-fours holding up the set in the back. You are simply creating a platform from which you will do your song and dance to sell your business idea to the world.

> TIP: *Use your money only to set up the business. Never use your own money to fund operations. If you can't get others to invest, your business is not worth starting.*

The Launch Phase

During the launch phase of your business, you are looking for working capital for items such as inventory, marketing, and salaries. You have put together a formal budget and you have tripled it. (I'm dead serious—whatever you think you need, triple it!) The reason I call it a launch phase is because similar to NASA, in this phase you need to equip your business with enough fuel, oxygen, and supplies to sustain it in space for the next twelve months—with no chance of refuelling. That means everything needs to have at least two or three backup systems. Because this approach requires a larger amount of capital, tens or hundreds of thousands of dollars, this is when you need three sources of capital—angels, equity, and debt. Angels can be anyone from your rich uncle to high net worth individuals among your circle of friends. Equity and debt are best sourced from a larger pool of high net worth individuals or investment funds. Depending on the amounts you require, you can raise money with the help of your lawyer via friends and family, or for larger amounts via an investment bank (more on them later).

The Five Investor Types

In my years of raising money, and in dealing with shareholders and investor relations, I've come to the conclusion that there are five categories of shareholders. In no particular order, they are *bipolar*, *spy*, *angel*, *friend*, and *shark*. Get to know these types by heart, because you only have twenty minutes in your investor pitch to figure out which type of investor he or she is.

Bipolar

The bipolar investor is the type of guy who will call you one day absolutely happy with the progress you're making, and then call you the following day yelling down the phone with all the swear words in the dictionary. They are the ones who send you nasty emails every time you've hit a fantastic milestone and you put out a press release. They whine and complain and make your life hell, but they won't take their money out because they know that they are either invested too deeply in your business, or they are actually happy with your performance but don't want you to know that. I've dealt with a shareholder who would take me to the brink of insanity and back with a simple phone call. And most of those phone calls started out praising all the good things I had done before continuing with those three wonderful words, "I am concerned." And then he would let me have it.

As a side note, I have found the phrase "I am concerned..." to be a fantastic way of getting one's point across and getting someone's attention. You will be amazed how easily you can manipulate people using these three little words.

Spy

The spy investor generally makes a very small minority invest-ment—sometimes in the ballpark of around $100,000. Their goal is not to help your company but rather to obtain information because they have a multimillion-dollar investment in one of your competi-tors. The key lesson here is not to take just anybody's money, but to weed out the spies from the start. Throughout the years, I've come to the realization at various times that things were being leaked to our competitors. Unfortunately, I realized too late. You now have an opportunity to make sure that the investors you bring on board are fully invested in you and not your competitors. Do as much home-work on them as they will do on you.

Angel

The third category of investor is the angel. This is an investor who is patient, most of the time a successful entrepreneur themselves, who invests not just in the business but in the management team you've assembled, and who believes in your capabilities. Angel investors are a very patient bunch. They understand the ups and downs of a young business, and time and again they will come to assist you in your time of need. They let you run your business and seldom interfere with your plans, but they will also make the time to answer questions and be a mentor to you. This is hands-down the most valuable investor any entrepreneur can have. We call it smart money.

Friend

The fourth category of investor is your friend. This can be anyone you know through your own circle of friends who has decided to put some money into your company, including a relative, family member, neighbour, associate, former colleague, or simply a good friend. Generally, the friend invests a small amount of money, but is aligned with you nonetheless. Most of the time these shareholders will be sitting quietly on the sidelines trusting you because they know you quite well, and very often these are also the types of people who even with their limited means will come in with a second round of investment because they support you and they see that you can meet your milestones.

Shark

Last but not least, the absolute most dangerous category of investor is the shark. These are the types of people who are waiting for you to make a mistake so that they can take you out ruthlessly, coldly, and without hesitation. It is their single goal to take the company away from you when you are down. And make no mistake, these people exist. They are out there and they are waiting. And most of the time they are disguised in the form of funds that look perfectly normal on the outside. But as I always say, trust your instinct to avoid them. If you lack the instinct, look for character traits such as overt friendliness without them ever giving you a sense of their true personality, probing and backdoor calls to your board, political manoeuvring to weaken your position, and a pattern of odd demands, particularly concerning terms of your shareholders agreement or their investment. If you sense that you're dealing with a shark, call their past investee companies to dig up some dirt before you let them invest.

To really drive home the point about the danger of this type of investor, I will give you a taste of my own experience with a shark.

In December 2005, my most recent startup company had been in operation for little over a year and a half. By Christmas, it had become very apparent that our company had burned through most of the cash we had raised from investors. With only $5,000 in the bank account, it was definitely crunch time for us, particularly because there were some new rules and regulations that required us to put massive cash deposits down with the local utility to get our wind farm connected to the grid. When I went back to my investors to give them the news, it became very clear who was my friend and who was a shark. With my back against the wall, one investor decided it was time to take me out. The way the offer was made was very cunning: he was willing to offer us $1 million in cash at a share price of one cent per share, coupled with the requirement for me to personally give up my entire share ownership in the company and some additional ludicrous provisions that were just there to dilute me out of my ownership.

The pressure that my father and I were under came to a peak at the Christmas dinner table with my mother in tears because I had been on the telephone for five hours trying to negotiate a deal with another group of investors. I was fortunate that most of my investors were angels who had gone through the same bullshit with their own businesses, so they rallied around me and helped me prevent disaster. Some people aren't so lucky and have ended up losing everything. Christmas 2005 was ruined, but the company was saved. Angels are the types of people who understand that not everything goes as planned, but they are willing to stick it out because they trust you and your management team. Angels are your best insurance policy against shark encounters. The best call I ever made was to tell the shark to go to hell. I also had the subsequent satisfaction of seeing the shark booted out of his own fund two years down the road.

Types of Capital

Equity

Equity is the issuance of common stock or any other security representing an ownership interest in your company. Beware of lonely individuals who will offer to help you raise money on a consulting/commission basis. Once again, most of these people are not qualified, nor are they registered as a securities broker. Always do background checks with the Financial Industry Regulatory Authority (FINRA) or the Investment Dealers Association (IDA) if you are in Canada. FINRA is the largest independent regulator for all securities firms doing business in the United States. They oversee nearly 4,535 brokerage firms, 163,620 branch offices, and 631,640 registered securities representatives. On their website (www.finra.org) you will find the BrokerCheck tool, a free tool to help you research the professional backgrounds of current and former FINRA-registered brokerage firms and brokers. It should be the first resource you turn to when choosing whether to start or continue doing business with a particular broker.

Debt

When you start a business, no bank will lend you money unless you put a personal guarantee on your line of credit, normally encumbering your house, your credit, or some other collateral. I have found this to be too risky for my own liking. I suggest you avoid this at all cost. Never risk the welfare of your family or your home, and all the things that you have worked so hard to attain in life. But my businesses are more complex and significantly more capital intensive than a typical small business startup, so it is up to you to make this determination.

The general rule with a bank is that, as an entrepreneur, you will be unable to get any sort of financing. Most banks or loan companies that provide lines of credit or loans look for at least three years of financial statements, preferably audited. Because your business does not have a track record, banks are going to be unwilling to lend you money unless you provide a personal guarantee. If you have an asset such as a house, you could put up that asset as a guarantee against the loan for your business. But I highly recommend not doing this for the reasons stated above. Furthermore, to extend you a line of credit, most banks require 100 percent security. For example, if you want a $50,000 line of credit, you have to provide a $50,000 cash deposit to be held in trust with the bank. This might establish a credit record for your company, but it doesn't actually infuse new working capital into your business, and this guideline was in place before the financial crisis of 2008 that has turned into an ongoing recession and still exists at the time of this writing in 2012. Today banks are even less likely to lend you money, so you have to find creative ways to fund your business. Banks are not in the business of lending money to start-ups anyway. The sooner you come to that realization, the quicker you can find other means of financing elsewhere.

One more important note: Never, ever get loans from loan sharks, pawn shops, or high interest sources, even if they may look semi-legitimate. It is not worth the risk and the stress. These people are in the business of keeping you in debt, and most of the time the sources of these funds are highly questionable. If you are going to take on debt, it's best to source it from your local bank or through a registered investment dealer, also known as an investment bank or broker. I have heard a lot about crowd-sourcing via the Internet. This is where a large group of people give a small amount of money towards a larger loan, but again the terms of the loans can be very harsh.

Hybrid Debt

As dangerous as debt is to a startup, there is another form of debt called a convertible debenture, which might be more beneficial because it has some unique conversion features. It is essentially a debt instrument that can be converted into stock by the holder. These can be secured or unsecured against assets of your business, or a floating first charge of security on the entire business. By adding the convertibility option, the issuer pays a lower interest rate on the loan compared to what would be paid if there was no option to convert. You can also negotiate the interest payments to be made in the form of stock, which can reduce your default risk quite dramatically. You can use these instruments to obtain the capital you need to grow or maintain your business at an earlier stage than would otherwise be possible by raising equity. But remember, this is still debt. Very often, these debt instruments contain clauses that require lender consent on certain business transactions—which leaves you open to some negotiation risk. Generally, a private lender will want something in return for approving the deal, and that's where things can get expensive and time consuming. Because of the conversion feature, the document is quite expensive to draft. In my experience, debentures are the most expensive form of money because of the time and effort that goes into negotiations and legal work. The first $250,000 dollars I ever raised was in the form of a convertible debenture with an investment fund that later converted the loan into equity when we went public.

Hoard your cash

The biggest mistake I see entrepreneurs make is that the second they have money in the bank they go on a spending spree. As an entrepreneur, you got into this business because you wanted to get more cash in your bank account. Now that someone has given you money, you want to show that you are successful, so you go and buy that brand new office furniture suite, the bells-and whistles photocopier, the overpriced secretary and the fancy company car. There is only one problem. You didn't *earn* that money; it was entrusted to you by people who believed in your idea and your personal abilities to execute on your business plan.

My business partners and I have seen this on many occasions consulting for various startups. The sheer stupidity of some entrepreneurs has led some really promising companies to go under before they ever had a chance to get off the ground. The successful new record label that went insolvent because of mismanagement of funds and the Voice-over-IP company that was about to challenge Ma Bell went of business because of an out of control spending spree by the principal to furnish his new office space. We have seen it all. In fact, that is partly why we got out of consulting altogether; we were sick and tired of people not heeding our warnings.

When I start a business, I start it from the ground up. My approach has always been to hoard as much cash as I possibly can. I do this by limiting staff, keeping a low profile, paying contract wages rather than salaries, sharing office space, and stretching out our payments to suppliers. I require my CFOs to have fantastic people skills. They need to be able to manage suppliers and pay bills late and get away with it. How they do it always amazes me, but it is a much needed startup skill. When we would get an invoice that was due within thirty days, my CFOs would somehow manage to pay the bill off over a period of six months. Now that's stretching the dollar. Our CFOs do this by managing our relationships with suppliers, including managing their expectations, being loyal, and playing a bit of the good cop/bad cop routine between our suppliers and us. Of course, you can only do this for so long until you have to pony up the money. But for the first three years, it's a critical tactic. And it works. Always ask for a payment plan.

Pay yourself first

When you start a business, figure out the minimum salary you need to survive. Set up your payroll systems and raise enough money to last you for a year. No matter how many creditors call or knock on your door, no matter how important the letter sounds that lands on your desk, always and without failure pay yourself and your employees first. This is a golden rule. It comes from personal experience.

By paying yourself first, you ensure that your focus is on the business at hand, not whether you can pay your mortgage. Running your own business is all about focus. If you can focus your efforts on solving the money problems of your business, you will find a solution. If you have to deal with your personal finances on top of that, forget it. And the reason why you need to pay your employees first is to build and maintain loyalty. As a business owner your primary responsibility is to shield your employees from the harsh realities of the business world. If people know that they will get paid and know they are taken care of, they will go through fire with you, even in times of crisis. Never in my life have I asked my employees to skip a payday, ever. Make it a golden rule.

Your banking relationship

I have a love/hate relationship with the banks, partially because they have rarely loaned me money when I needed it, and when they have loaned, there has always been some fine print that allows them to change the terms in their favor. Furthermore, in my early years of being an entrepreneur, I had some snooty customer service rep close a business bank account on me for accidentally bouncing one single check. I learned a lesson out of that.

But I have learned that two banking relationships are critical to being a successful entrepreneur. The first is your relationship with your personal banker, and the second is your relationship with the branch manager of your company's main bank.

You might be thinking, *wait a second—I don't have a million dollars to be able to qualify for a personal banker.* That's not what I mean by a personal banker. What I mean is you need a person at your bank, preferably two, who you can call for assistance. This is someone who can help cushion the blow even if your financial outlook is bleak. When I was nine years old and opened my first account, my father introduced me to his customer service/relationship manager, Karen. I am happy to say that I have known Karen for over twenty-four years. I have moved to subsequent branches together with her (I think somewhere in the neighbourhood of five times). Even though she is now a retired manager of a branch, I still stay in touch with her, in particular when it comes to critical items. It is imperative that you have someone you can turn to, because undoubtedly you will get knocked about financially a couple of times. Karen stuck with me through my "stupid" years when I didn't know better than to bounce checks, get behind on my line of credit payments, even forcing her to close it on me and some other things of which I am not too proud. But I am grateful that I had someone like Karen in my life who helped me through many a rough patch. At the same time, I was always grateful for her help, and without fail I sent her a $100 Christmas gift basket—my own unique way of saying, "I know how stupid I am. Thank you for your patience; it is tremendously appreciated."

Your second relationship has to be with your branch manager at your business bank. I try not to mix the two for reasons of avoiding comingling. What I mean by that is that people have a very hard time separating your persona from your company. Just ask my controller; you wouldn't believe how many times people have billed the company for something that had absolutely nothing to do with business and vice versa. It just happened that my company shared the same name as me. Business bankers are not only there to help you with a transfer, but to help you work through the rough patches. I make it a point to update my bankers on a regular basis. I have never shied away from letting my branch manager know when we are going through some tough times or cash shortages, because the manager was always aware of the other side of the equation—every time I had a multi-million dollar amount in my bank account, the commercial arm of some competing bank would try and lure me away. But we stay. We are loyal. That trust and loyalty can pay off. And if you feel like you are not getting your money's worth, then just open a second bank account at another branch. See if they like you better there. In fact, when we start a new company, we normally open two or three bank accounts at various financial institutions because that way we can see how we like the people. But more importantly, once you start making money (i.e. three years of audited financial statements with a solid history of positive cash flows), you can ask three banks for a line of credit, instead of just one.

CHAPTER 5

Investment Bankers

An investment bank, also known as a securities dealer or broker, is a firm that assists businesses in raising debt and equity capital. Investment bankers are the used car sales people of Wall Street. They will promise you the world, charge you hidden fees, and then not deliver—or so people say. I have had quite a different experience. Most of my i-bankers have become great friends. Once again, it comes down to the importance of building relationships. My lawyer made a couple of calls to get me in touch with a boutique investment firm that had specialized expertise in raising money in the oil, gas, and mining sector and was looking to diversify into renewable energy. The reason I say boutique is because they were small enough to care, connected enough to raise money, and confident enough to put their own money at risk. They managed to help me raise in excess of $10 million over three years, and I made some friends along the way who helped me during those crunch times I mentioned previously.

How to Choose an Investment Banker

There are three things to consider when looking to engage an i-banker to help you raise capital:

1. What are the **commissions** and **fees** they charge?
2. What is their **hurdle rate**?
3. What is their relevant **expertise** and **track record** of closing deals in your industry or related industries?

Most i-bankers work on what is called a "best efforts" basis. Unlike an underwritten public offering where they take on risk, best efforts means that they will do their best to help you raise the money, but there are no guarantees. Most of the time they will also help you create proper financial models and presentations, and they will put a value on your company and the share price. You may not like that price, but it's probably what the current market is giving; furthermore, they know what their client base is looking for. Essentially, they will make the calls and set up the meetings for you. Since you have already created your **Staging Kit**, their reps will use this document to pitch on the phones and email on your behalf. Then it's up to you to impress at the meetings.

TIP: *A good i-bank can set up ten to twelve meetings per day— that's almost one meeting per hour. Subtract fifteen minutes of travel time to get to your next meeting, and this leaves you with only forty-five minutes max at each meeting. After a short introductory handshake, you have about twenty minutes to get through your power point presentation, ten minutes for questions and answers, five minutes to talk about terms, and you're off to the next guy. Now do you see why you can't have more than twelve slides?*

Commissions and Fees

For their services, i-bankers charge various fees. The four most common fees are as follows:

1. **A commission**, which is a cash percentage (usually anywhere from 8-12 percent) of the total amount raised.
2. **Warrants**, which give the i-banker the right to buy stock in your company at a pre-determined price, usually higher than the market value of the deal. Sometimes investors might ask for warrants as well, to sweeten the deal.
3. **Working fees**, which are fees i-bankers charge during the capital-raising effort or just prior to it. As far as I am concerned, this is a bullshit fee and you should do everything possible to avoid it. Increase the commission if you have to. But avoid upfront fees.
4. **Expenses**. Very often there are expenses associated with raising money—trip expenses, photocopies, and the list goes on. You should always require these to be pre-approved

by you, and expenses should always come out of the proceeds of the capital raised, never out of your pocket.

Hurdle Rates

When choosing an i-bank, you need to be aware of hurdle rates, both for the i-banker and their existing list of investor clients. What does that mean? A hurdle rate is a minimum threshold amount the i-bank can raise without losing money. Small deals are just as expensive as big deals. It takes as much effort to raise $1 million as it does to raise $100 million. So if you need $5 million, don't waste your time with i-bankers that have a $50 million hurdle rate. In fact, investment bankers will respect you for understanding this, so don't be afraid to ask. Even if they can't help you, you can always ask them for a referral to a smaller boutique firm with the promise of getting them in on your larger raise down the road.

The same goes for investors. When Warren Buffet announced to the world that he was looking to go green, I blatantly and without introduction sent him a letter asking him to invest $100 million in my wind farm. Much to my surprise, I got a phone call from him a week later. He said that he really liked the deal, but his hurdle rate was somewhere around $500 million for comparable deals. There was no way he could make an investment because he needed to focus his time on placing billions of dollars. Once again, it takes him the same amount of time for a small deal as it would for a large deal, but the large deal will have greater overall return on investment. Warren ended up making a $500 million investment in another wind project in the midwest. So always ask your i-banker about their hurdle rates.

Private investors excepted, many funds have limitations on the market cap or revenues of the investee company, whether it's public or private or the time to make an exit strategy. For example, you are meeting with Fund X. They need you to have sales of $10 million and go public in less than nine months. But you are raising your first million, and you have about $500,000 in sales so far and don't expect to go public for another two to three years. What chance do you have of getting their money? It's better to save that meeting for a year down the road when you have grander ambitions.

Expertise and Track Record

The final key element to choosing an ibanker is to understand their track record and expertise in the field. You have to think a bit outside of the box here. I'll give you an example. I chose an oil and gas boutique firm to raise money for my wind power business. Sounds somewhat odd, doesn't it? But to an investor in Texas, it's the same concept whether it's an oil well or a wind turbine producing a royalty on his land and the associated tax benefits. So the i-bank's expertise, track record, and contacts in oil and gas, and my ability to dumb down the idea of a wind farm (KISS principle) made for a perfect combination. Try to think of a cross-industry combination in terms of your business. People love pigeonholing a business. If you can expand your horizon to find similar business processes, even in a completely unrelated business, you stand a better chance of raising money. On the other hand, be careful when choosing a firm that has all your competitors as their clients. Working with such a firm is never a good idea, because they already have a relationship with your competitors, and the last thing you want is for you to get less attention from your i-bankers than your competition gets.

TIP: *There is a difference between an i-bank's "order book" and funds in the bank account. If an i-banker says to you, "Our order book is at $2.3 million," that doesn't mean they have closed the investor; it's just a so-called soft-circle sale. The order book is full of non-firm commitments. So once you've hooked an investor, be ruthless about getting him to sign the documents and send his money. Work with the representative that took you to the meeting to get the guy to close. The longer it takes, the higher the risk that he won't convert from the order book to a closed deal.*

CHAPTER 6

Your Management Team

Investing in Your Team

Investors don't invest in your business; they invest in you, your team, and your collective track record. If this is your first venture, this can be a very tough nut to crack because of two reasons. First, when you first start a business, you are always cash strapped, and it is very hard to pay someone with a limited amount of money in the bank account. Second, you have to find like-minded individuals who are willing to share the vision and the risk, work for less money

Walking on Water

than they could possibly earn elsewhere, but perhaps get a share of the company. So we need to spend some time designing your management team.

Managing for Success

I'm a big believer in giving people ownership in your business. It is a big motivator for someone who wants to leave the corporate grind to be involved in a startup but who needs to get over the fear of potentially risking his paycheck. The biggest reason is that, once they are owners, people will be a bit more careful with how they treat your business and how they spend the company's money. Always hire people who are smarter than you. It's true that people feel threatened very easily by co-workers. In most companies, managers end up hiring people who are dumber than they are, just to make sure they don't lose their own job. But as an entrepreneur, you can't have that worry. In fact, you are in desperate need of people who are smarter than you and have a longer track record than you have. You're the boss, you own the company, so go ahead—hire people who are smarter than you, because no matter how good you are, there is always an opportunity for learning something new. Your investors will see this trait as an asset. In the following chapters, I will give you additional ideas on how to get people on your team to bolster your company's track record.

Delegate but Maintain Oversight

One major problem that afflicts startups is the money-raising cycle. You spend all your time raising money, and then you go and work for a couple of months on your business, only to realize you need

50

more money. You drop everything and make another round to various sources, asking for more. The risk is that sometimes you run out of money faster than you can raise it. That is when most founders get into trouble. In order to avoid this trap you need to be out there raising money consistently and throughout the year—particularly while you are cash flow negative. To do this you will need to delegate the work to capable people in your company, freeing up your time to raise money. But delegating is not an easy task for an entrepreneur.

I hate bosses. It's probably one of the biggest reasons why I quit my job very early on in my career and became self-employed. You probably feel the same way—you want to be in control of your destiny. But be warned. Now you are on the other side, and there is nothing worse than a boss that looks over your shoulder at every moment and doesn't give you the freedom to make decisions or grow in your position. The biggest problem you will face is learning to delegate work to others. I learned that lesson too late. I was quite obsessed with having to control everything, or doing it to my exacting standards, which I admit are very high. But I completely ignored my private life and ended up gaining forty pounds. I found out the hard way: when I realized I was running out of breath while trying to keep up with Sir Richard Branson on his personal tour around the hills of Necker Island. That was a definite sign to me that I was doing something wrong. Here was a man who owns two hundred companies and employs more than ten thousand people; yet he was in shape and had enough time to stay in shape, and he even had time to give a nobody like me a tour of the entire island.

I have learned that if you are patient with people, they will learn from their mistakes and can grow into your shoes. But it takes some time and mentoring. Don't be afraid to give work to others— you might be surprised how people thrive. Empower them to make decisions, even if that means the occasional mistake. Get them excited about the company's vision, and remember that they also have a personal life and career ambitions, so cater to those needs as a boss. You will be rewarded through increased productivity.

There are also fantastic ways of outsourcing work to third parties in India. Yes you heard right: India. It's called a virtual assistant. I could never really justify a full-time assistant in North America. Most of them just sat around the office staring at the ceiling because I really never needed anyone to check my email or answer my phones. I was good enough at avoiding people on my own. But there were certain tasks that easily could be outsourced, such as expense reports, follow up calls, making sure my housekeeper has all the supplies she needs, and so on. It of course takes a little courage to overcome the fear of giving your personal information to someone in India, but there are a couple of very reputable companies like Brickwork India that do a fantastic job at this. Rates start anywhere from $10 to $25 per hour, depending on whether you need a lonely assistant or a PhD.

Family vs. Friends vs. New Hires

One way to get around this dilemma is by hiring family or friends, but this is a tricky subject because you are intermingling two worlds, your private life and your business life. You need to strike a balance between cheap labor and overloading yourself to the point of turning your company into a family business that stands no chance of raising money.

Working together with family members has its benefits and disadvantages. You can expect business to be talked over the dinner table during the annual holidays—something that even my mom frowned upon. And it is very difficult making business decisions when you have family interests to consider. Most family members might also find it difficult to draw a line between business and family, and that can lead to conflict. I am very fortunate that I have been able to work with my father. And I would venture to say that this has been one of the most rewarding things I have had the privilege of experiencing in my life. It represents a 180-degree turn from my early twenties when my father and I weren't necessarily on the best of terms. My dad is pretty much the only person I know who can pull rank and lecture me. But he does it behind closed doors, and we always show a united front and manage to come to a resolution, which shows the deep respect we have for each other. His career experience certainly managed to accelerate my own, but hiring your parents is not for the faint hearted, so think twice before you do so.

Of the five friends I hired, only one managed to balance work and personal relationships. All the others I ended up letting go (firing!) because it didn't work out. Of course, that did some temporary damage to my friendships with these people. I was fortunate that we had a good enough friendship to eventually overcome this hiccup in our relationship. So generally, I would recommend staying away from the temptation to hire friends or to go into business with them.

Hiring outside of your company can be a hit-or-miss prospect, too, and most of the time it turns out to be a miss. I like hiring people from within my companies and giving them brand new projects that they have absolutely no qualifications for whatsoever. I do this mostly because I am already convinced of their abilities to learn on the fly, to make decisions, and to accept a challenge. Otherwise, they wouldn't be working for me. Plus, it's cheaper than paying a large placement fee to a human resource agency. I have had only one or two successes using a placement firm, and these people are with me today. Most others I found myself or met in some other capacity, such as a consultant who just happened to impress me enough for me to offer a job. I have found that to be the easiest and least expensive way to find the right employees. If there is a consultant you like, hire that person and make him/her an offer. You would be surprised at how many people will accept an offer of employment simply because you wrote them an email and said you were interested in hiring them. That's because most of them can't stand staying at a consulting firm longer than a couple of years by that time, they've learned everything they can and are itching to leave. But as consultants, they are also used to the ups and downs of cash flow and the need to chase business, something a startup struggles with on a daily basis.

Mistakes Will Happen

I give my employees enormous amounts of autonomy and decision making capabilities, knowing full well that I might get stuck with a bad decision that will cost me money. But the benefits far outweigh the risks. Some people are a little uneasy at first, because they expect a boss that micromanages, only to realize that most of the time I am not even in the office because I am chasing the next business opportunity. They sometimes get scared, or walk into my office saying, "I'm not doing anything; is there something wrong?" My usual reply to them is, "Well, you know why I hired you, right?" The answer is inevitably, "Yes, of course!" I then counter and say, "Then I suggest perhaps you ask your new coworkers to get you up to speed so you can figure out where you can jump in and pick up the slack." If I have done a good job at hiring, then that person will be extremely busy within about two weeks, because he or she take on projects and justify his/her position.

When it comes to making mistakes, ultimately my rule is that everyone gets one chance. You are allowed one major mistake.

Indeed, I have had employees cost me a quarter of a million dollars because they made a mistake, but I didn't fire them. This is because I know full well that I have made mistakes in the past, and if I fire them, I have wasted $250,000 training them. Rest assured, they won't make that mistake ever again in their entire life. And if they make it while working at my company, they know to pack up their stuff. Fortunately, that has never happened yet.

Company Culture and Work Atmosphere

I have had some really bad experiences when it comes to corporate culture. Gossiping, backstabbing, micromanaging bosses, discriminatory attitudes, bosses who don't keep their word when it comes to paying your bonus, and the list goes on and on. That's why I ventured out on my own to start with. I couldn't stand it anymore.

When I launched my first company, I made sure that company culture would be more important than company profitability. You might think that is absurd, but in the end, if your employees are happy and motivated, they will go the extra mile to make sure the company makes a profit—because they care.

The first thing I emphasized was a zero tolerance policy for discrimination. If I hear even the slightest negative remark out of a person's mouth in relation to ethnicity, sexual orientation, gender discrimination, or religion—even if it's an ill-timed joke—that person is fired…on the spot…no ifs, ands, or buts. All my employees know this, every single one. And because of it, nobody does it. It's that simple.

Secondly, I motivate employees by giving them extra vacation time (six weeks to be precise), and every now and then they will find a little gift on their desk. It might be a Starbucks gift card, free movie tickets, or a prepaid gas card. Because you're the business owner, these gifts don't have to cost you money. I use our corporate credit card, which has a rewards points feature. I will take some large expense, charge it to the card, and have enough points for the rest of the year to use for employee gifts. It's the little things that make the difference. Instead of that dreaded office birthday cake, I take people to the local theme park, movie matinees, boat cruises or the local art museum. And I never, ever plan it in advance. I always make it a surprise announcement; I don't really care how busy you are. Everybody goes, including the receptionist. We just lock the door. The world won't stop turning because we don't answer our phones. But the effect on company culture and work atmosphere doubles productivity and just makes it a great place to work. There is more to working there than just a salary.

CHAPTER 7

Lawyers, Accountants, And Auditors

Quick question: If I were to ask you, "Who is your lawyer?" what would you reply?

If you answered, "I have Bob so-and-so, a friend of the family. I can call him if I need him," then you are in trouble. You need a lawyer, right now. But let me tell you why.

Most young and inexperienced entrepreneurs that I have met have told me they don't need a lawyer right this minute. But if you are renting an office, leasing a store, buying a franchise, or selling a product, you need someone to look over the contracts. Contracts are never there for the good times. They are there for the times when the "shit hits the fan" so to speak. When you are in disagreement with someone, when you are being cornered, or when someone tries to pull a fast one on you, contracts lay out all the terms that you as an entrepreneur cannot even begin to comprehend. But more importantly, lawyers, by the sheer nature of feeling the pressure to bill hours, are a very connected bunch. They go to luncheons, cocktail parties, seminars, and networking events. These are events that you as an entrepreneur generally don't have the time for, nor the cash to attend. Your lawyer can get you connected and can be a source of contacts when you need them.

Finding a Lawyer

Lawyers are expensive, and many will charge you enough to clear out your bank account before you have even started your business. But if you find the right one, it can be a rewarding experience. When I started my record label, I was using the wrong set of tools. I decided that I would work with the best law firm in the entertainment industry. I chose the lawyer by a click through the list of lawyers on their website: bad mistake. My first experience with lawyers ended up costing me over $30,000, nearly bankrupting me before I got started, which was partially responsible for the debt I had. I think I still owe money to them, although they haven't tried to collect it—yet.

My first mistake was that I didn't look to build a relationship with a good lawyer. My second mistake was that I didn't really get along with my lawyer, and my third mistake was that the person I thought was the best lawyer really wasn't.

By now you should have gotten a sense that the art of business is based on relationships—good relationships. The same goes for your lawyer. When I started my power Company, I decided I was going to get the right people on board from the beginning. So I figured

I'd work my way down from the top. I knew I was going to take the company public eventually, which meant I needed a corporate and/or securities lawyer. I then asked myself who would know the most and be the best. I decided to cold call the head of the Toronto Stock Exchange. If not he, then who else? Right? After a couple of unsuccessful attempts to reach him, my persistence paid off. After a short conversation about my grand ambitions, he was kind enough to provide me with a list of four individuals he personally recommended. Now, something peculiar happens when you name-drop top officials or people of authority. When I called the four lawyers in question and mentioned that they had been personally recommended to me by the head of the Toronto Stock Exchange, I not only got their interest, but I also managed to squeeze in not just one, but two or three free meetings with them. Of course, every time I met them I had prepared one or two questions I needed answering. So while I shopped for a lawyer, I also managed to get some good advice—free of charge. Even though I met all four lawyers, I really only liked one of them.

Fortunately for me, I have always been able to rely on my gut feeling when it comes to judging people's true nature. But more importantly, I knew that I would have to like the person I would be working with.

In situations where you don't have a gut feeling about a lawyer, there is a series of questions you should always ask yourself after your first meeting:

"Would I invite him/her to my house for dinner with the family?"

"Would I ask him/her to watch my kids (dog/cat)?"

Third, but most importantly, "If I'm completely broke, wasted, in jail, passed out in a puddle of my own vomit, would he/she be the person that I would want to bail me out? If so, can he/she do it in less than an hour?"

If the answer is yes to all three, great; it looks like you will get along. If you are not so sure, make some more calls and meet some more lawyers.

I am fortunate that I have a relationship like that with my corporate and securities lawyer Robert and my general legal counsel Wayne. I'm sure that they would not only bail me out, but would probably buy me a new shirt and put me up for the night. Fortunately, to date they have never had to do that.

When you have found the lawyer who is perfect for you, be loyal to him; help him drive his own business by giving out referrals; follow him if he chooses to go to another law firm. But take it a step further. Be a friend if and when they need your help.

Congrats, You Have Just Been Served

I was in New York attending a United Nations Global Compact Conference on CEOs fighting corruption when I happened to find myself at one of New York City's finest eateries sitting beside none other than Donald Trump. Somehow, we landed on the topic of lawsuits, and he said to me, "You can measure your success by the amount of times you get sued." That anecdote from the Donald has stuck with me ever since, and based on my personal experience, I agree with him.

Unless you are a crook, most lawsuits happen because of egos—someone was outshone by your deal making skills, has a false sense of entitlement, or thinks he can get away with grabbing money from you.

When you become successful and money starts flowing, you will get sued. It's a fact of life. Either people are trying to screw you over for their own selfish reasons, or they feel as if they have been cheated out of their own fortune and that somehow you are at fault. The problem with legal wrangling is that it can cripple you. It can stifle your day-to-day concentration on your work. That is why it is important to be prepared by having a good lawyer, so that when the time comes, you can hand off the details to him or her. That person for me is my long-time friend, business partner, and Director of Corporate Affairs, Wayne. He has been through the highs and lows with me, and he always watches my back. I can just pass things off to him knowing that they will get resolved one way or the other.

The Five Stages

The first time I was told on the phone that I would be served a statement of claim, I was in total disbelief that something like this could actually happen to a good guy like me. I have never done anything wrong. I'm a good person, right? That soon turned to paranoia. I started avoiding public spaces and didn't show up at my office for about four weeks, trying to avoid the process server. I simply couldn't handle the stress. I figured if I avoided getting served, I wouldn't have to deal with it. It got so bad I was literally paralyzed by my own fear. I couldn't work anymore. I was done. When I finally came to my senses and accepted the document, my fear turned into raging anger at the claims being thrown at me. Lawyers have a fantastic way of twisting words to make a payment dispute sound like capital murder. I read the document several times. In fact, I was so angry that I couldn't sleep for two days because of it. If you have ever been served, you've probably experienced this. It happens because in your mind, you are already in the courtroom defending your honor with every bit of ammunition that you can possibly think of. That's when I started coming to my senses and used calm, rational thinking to hand it off to someone who does this for a living.

Hand It Off

This is the point when your lawyers should come into play. After my psychosis ended I handed the document to my consigliore Wayne. He made it go away within two weeks. I was amazed. Defending my honor in the courtroom was no longer needed. The next time somebody sued me, I handed the document to Wayne without even opening it. I figured I would worry only if he was worried. In fact, these days we make a game of it; we see how much we can piss off the other side before they cave from the stress.

Knowing When to Settle

Going to court or arbitration is never fun, but more importantly, it sucks the life out of you and your company and wastes countless hours, incurs a tremendous amount of legal bills, and doesn't do anything to further your business. I have made it a rule to set dollar amounts for my various businesses whereby we automatically try to settle the dispute simply by sitting down with the other party and hammering out a deal. Most of the time, other business people will be reasonable because they understand the laws of diminishing legal returns just as much as you do. Of course, there will always be the occasional asshole who thinks he is better than you are, and with those guys, I show absolutely no mercy. I have been known to "release the hounds" on occasion.

Accountants and Auditors

Aside from lawyers, accountants and auditors are the single largest expense of doing business. I opted right from the start to go with one of the large auditing firms, simply because I wanted to look bigger and more successful than I was (yet), and because I was raising significant sums of money. I also went right away for audited financial statements, because that's what most people want to hear. Get someone to do your bookkeeping, and let a big firm do the audit. At the beginning, when things are simple, it shouldn't cost the world, but it will get you closer to that minimum of three years of audited financials so that you can get that bank line of credit. So start from year one, even if you haven't started your actual operations. It's very easy to audit a company with a zero balance sheet. Also, don't be afraid to fire them if they are screwing you on their fees. I fired one of the big three and replaced them with Deloitte after my first year because they came up with some dumb excuse to triple their audit fees. But don't do it too often, because it looks suspicious. Deloitte was excruciatingly expensive, but they always got the job done, were always fair, worked with me when I couldn't pay the bill on time, including taking equity, and eventually took my company public. That's about as good as it's going to get with an auditor.

CHAPTER 8

Doing Your Homework

In order to satisfy the requirements of an investor and your business plan, you will need to conduct some initial research into the industry demographics that your company will be selling in. Once you have a general understanding and have raised sufficient funds, you can then hire a marketing person who can put together the proper marketing plan and product mix. Keep in mind that here we are only concerned with setting the stage for you to raise money.

Market Research

For about ten years, I lived in the Fashion District in Toronto, better known as King & Bathurst by the locals. Over the years, I noticed that a particular shop location seemed to be changing hands on several occasions. First it was empty, then it was a PC store, then a clothing shop, then empty, and then another clothing shop. Each time, within months it would be shuttered with a notice on the door by the landlord that the lease wasn't paid. Right across the street, in my building, there was another storefront. It had always been a fast food place. First it was Mexican, then a falafel place, then a wing place, and now it's an Indian food place. The only person who ever made money was the landlord because he kept renting to new people. For years I wondered why there was so much turnover on this street, and then I realized what was happening. For each new business owner, their timing was off and the location was off. Our neighborhood didn't need a fashion store because we didn't shop in our neighborhood (contrary to its name), and the food place was in a location where the market was not big enough to support yet another restaurant crowding into an area that already had a Subway, McDonald's, Quiznos and eight other restaurants. Couple that with a location that was not as prominent as the others, and you have a recipe for disaster. The last store that was in there was a toy store. At one point they got so desperate they started selling ice cream. Now why would you put a toy store in an area full of young, single, career-oriented people? If you learn one thing from this little anecdote—it's to do your marketing homework.

I have spent hundreds of thousands of dollars researching new business opportunities and identifying market niches, only to walk away from the idea and find something elsewhere. But I see it as the cost of an education in a particular business or industry. I'd rather spend $100,000 learning about the aviation business than lose $100 million of investor money in an ill-timed launch of a new airline, as much as my ego really wanted that.

So how do you go about doing proper market research? This is where I like outsourcing things. There is no better person to research an industry than an MBA or PhD in economics who will give you a PowerPoint presentation that will knock your socks off. You couldn't do a better job. Companies like Brickwork India (www.brickworkindia.com) specialize in this, or you can always try www.guru.com. Take that information and see how it is relevant to your business and formulate a business strategy from it. Then test your theory with people who are willing to put their money where their mouth is. Forget about focus groups; test the sale, or if it's a retail idea, take a folding chair, sit outside of the store location you are considering renting, and then count pedestrians who walk by. Look at their demographics, see what they buy, where they are coming from and where they are going to, and ask them to answer a quick survey. That's called proper market research, which you should always do before you ever risk your startup capital on a dumb idea that may never work, no matter how good you think your product or service is.

Your Brand

Entrepreneurs are somewhat deranged. We think that people want something, when in fact they don't. Or perhaps they want something else. One of my best friends is currently the senior marketing manager at American Express. Her illustrious career has included being the brand manager at the Body Shop, T-Fal and the Heart and Stroke Foundation. Every time I go off on some entrepreneurial tangent in a marketing brainstorming session, she tells me, "It's not about you; it's about your customers."

Because we are creating a stage here, the whole branding exercise can be left to a later point until you have secured sufficient capital to do a proper brand architecture. Generally, a proper brand strategy done with an advertising agency will set you back about $40,000 to $70,000. A well-designed website will cost somewhere between $8,000 to $12,000 (or buy one at www.templatemonster. com for $60). Business cards and company brochures cost about $2,000 to $5,000 to print up (or get them for $25 at 123print.

com). So keep that in mind when you are developing your budget. And these are costs that should absolutely not be avoided because you are not a marketing expert. That's why they get paid the money they do. They will figure out what the consumer wants and how to relay your message in a cohesive and organized fashion.

CHAPTER 9

Strategy

The Value of Plan A, B, C, D, and E

Starting a business is like driving a sports car at 200 miles an hour down the road towards a brick wall and it's your job to swerve around the wall. The problem is that someone at the other end keeps pushing the wall from side to side. It is therefore imperative that you come up with a very good strategy plan that contemplates alternate scenarios. Experts call it game theory. I prefer to call it plan A, B, C, D, and E. My team and I would play out each possible scenario and have our plan A as the main goal in the main strategy. But we would always have a backup plan B and plan C. The reason you need to do this is to make sure that in any potential scenario, you will always have a way out or a way forward. You need to run through the motions in order to be prepared for anything that entrepreneurship can throw at you, and most of the time these plans will revolve around money—where you are going to get it from, what you are going to do if you run out, and how you are going to spend it if you're short. Rest assured your business never turns out how you plan it. You might have to make some very difficult decisions, such as layoffs, salary deferrals, or shuttering the business. So be prepared. Do not whitewash the risks. I have seen too many people underestimate the environment they're in, and sadly, they went under. Don't be one of them.

The credit crisis of 2007 to 2009 was a very good example of our plan in action. Building wind farms takes a significant amount of capital; generally, anywhere in the ballpark of $40 million to $100 million. When the banks stopped lending, we had no way of getting debt financing for projects, but we had a Plan B.

Plan B for us was to set up partnerships with existing investors who had lots of money or a long track record. Coupled with our own experience, this allowed us to get the financing we needed from banks around the world. Plan C would kick in if that particular equity partner we had chosen wasn't ready, willing, or able to make the investment, which meant we would have a third investor lined up already as a backup. At the time, three of my largest competitors went bankrupt, but my business survived the credit crisis, and we were only one of a handful of developers that were building in 2009. It was solely because we had thought through our strategy and had multiple action plans in case something went wrong.

CHAPTER 10

Growing Your Business

Letting Go of Your Baby

There comes a time when your company moves beyond your little bachelor pad, beyond the virtual office in the high rise, and becomes a real business with a real office and real employees. It eventually grows so much in size that the founder has to seriously consider bringing in the big guns: senior management. Although it was easy for me to make this decision, others find it hard to face the reality that the team that started the business might not necessarily be the best team to grow the business or take it to the next level. My first CFO was good at managing the cash of a startup, but once we exceeded the level of having $1.2 billion worth of development projects under management, major cracks in the system started to show. She was stressed out, accounts were a mess, and the auditors were getting frustrated that it took six months to finish a year-end report. Similarly, I realized that I was a good manager, but by no means did I have the knowledge or experience to run a public company, and I knew that's where I wanted to head—having a listing on a Stock Exchange. That's when I made the call to hire a CEO and a new CFO, and both had experience running a public company. More importantly, I really didn't want to stick my head out into the public markets, but preferred that a CEO have that responsibility. Perhaps it was because so many CEOs were being sued by shareholders at the time, and some were even going to prison. All I knew was that the liability was just too great for me.

So finding my new team was my first move. My second move was to lay off people who were not only my friends, but who had worked very hard in making this little startup survive. Unfortunately, they had now become a liability, and their inexperience could take down the entire operation. That is sometimes the tough part about being an entrepreneur—the really difficult decisions always rest with you.

When you are hiring a CEO, you need to be very careful of who you pick. I made the mistake of hiring someone who had good credentials, but whose personality didn't jive with the company culture. I never really got along with him either. Did he make the right decisions for my business? Yes, absolutely. Could he have gone about it differently? Definitely. A year after going public, our disagreements came to a head during a one-on-one meeting during which we came to the decision that it was time for him to go, but not before we closed our largest deal: the sale of my now public company to a larger NASDAQ listed company in the US. This provided him a gracious exit while achieving an above market exit strategy for my shareholders. Because I knew that he is a bit of a pit bull, however, I asked him to be on the board of the new company, knowing that he would represent my interests within the new owners' organization. To this day, we stay in contact, and we have found mutual respect for our respective talents.

Boosting Sales

In the words of the late sales guru Chet Holmes, the biggest secret to business sales success is "pigheaded discipline and determination." Chet has a tendency to take things to the extreme, but there is a certain truth in that. If there is one sales book, you should read, it's "The Ultimate Sales Machine" by Chet Holmes. I believe that you have to think of yourself as a business owner rather than someone running a business. Sales cannot be learned. Either you are a super sales person, or you are not. If you are not, then hire them. Make sure to work this into your "who you are" strategy we discussed in the first chapter.

If you are to build a large and successful company, you should be working on sales strategy, not making the actual sale. Most people forget to differentiate between strategy and tactics.

Sales tactics are the things you do to generate sales, such as ads, attending trade shows, your website, a brochure, a press release, a sales call, and so on.

Sales strategy has to do with your long-term goals, the overall impact you want your business to have, and the ultimate perception you'd like your clients to have about you.

Reread the last two sentences. Do it now. Most people don't understand the difference. Most people also don't understand the sales process or the steps in a sales situation.

The seven steps of every sales situation are as follows:

1. Establish rapport
2. Find the need
3. Build value
4. Create desire (make them want it)
5. Overcome objections
6. Close the sale
7. Follow up

Mastering the first two steps will get you 65 percent of the way toward closing the sale. Understanding your customers' needs and establishing rapport with them on a certain level will tip the probability of making the sale in your favor. You need to practice this skill with your entire team, again and again.

> TIP: *The secret to making sales doesn't come from using four thousand different tactics, but rather perfecting seven tactics and doing them four thousand times—and then further concentrating them on the top one hundred customers that drive the most revenue for your company.*

The following goals should be your strategic objectives in any sales interaction:

1. You want to be trusted, respected, and well liked.
2. You want to be admired, and you want to be perceived as much more of an expert in your field than any of your competitors are.
3. You want to have great influence with your clients, and to have a pre-emptive strategy that keeps customers from

believing when competitors say anything negative against you

4. You are bold enough to broach the topic of price comparisons right up front.

5. You have a referral strategy in place for every single conversation.

6. You are able to communicate a brand loyalty strategy.

7. Be able to convey that your company has an education-based sales and marketing strategy.

8. Know exactly what you want to achieve with every sales call.

The key to defeating any competitor, even if they offer a lower price, is to be seen as an expert. People will always pay more for an expert. At one of his seminars, Chet gave me a good example for how to think about approaching one's customers. He said to imagine that all your potential customers are sitting in a giant stadium, and you have the opportunity to present your sales pitch to all of them all at once. What would be the title of your speech?

Along those same lines, how many of the objectives listed above can you achieve? Keep in mind that in order to drive sales you need to "sell the store" rather than the product. What that means is that you need to build brand loyalty on purpose.

Using market data in the sales process is absolutely key. If you have done proper research about the industry your business is in, you should be well-armed with statistics and data that can support your product sales pitch. What underlying data do you have that set the buying criteria in your favor and motivate buyers to buy now?

All great companies are masters of strategy, and they have tactics to meet the needs of their strategies. They have mastered the art of getting clients, as well as the art of communicating on the phone and the web, and they use effective presentations and visual aids with underlying data that creates motivation. They have learned the value of goal setting, following up, setting minimum performance levels, and hiring superstar sales people. There are numerous books that can help you in this area. Whatever you do, master the art of the sale.

Transitioning

As we talked about in an earlier chapter, there are two key phases when you launch your business: the *idea stage* and the *launch phase*. But there is an important third phase, which I call the *transition phase*. It's the time when your business starts taking flight and pressure cracks begin to show. That's when you need to act fast to ensure the company doesn't implode.

At the beginning, it's just you sitting behind a desk in your home office. And it generally takes two years before you can move out of that home office and hire employees. That's because you won't have enough cash flow to hire enough people. As you become more successful, you will find yourself hiring like a mad man just to keep up with demand. In this transitional phase, you are still a small company, and you are still personally responsible for a lot of the work. You will do more work than you had ever imagined possible. That is because you are training new people and catching their mistakes while trying to complete your own duties. You do it all because you enjoy your work and have a passion for your business. The major problem is that things start falling through the cracks. They might be small at first, but before you know it, major disasters appear on the horizon. That's when frustration kicks in and you realize things aren't working out, not to mention you no longer have a personal or family life.

I have found that the only way to keep up with the demands of an entrepreneurial enterprise, and now running multiple companies, is to make sure that you are well organized. That doesn't mean you have to have a tidy desk and everything has to line up perfectly. By no means does my desk ever look clean. My method is the chaos method. It works for me. However, I use what's called the Rapid Planning Method, which was developed by Anthony Robbins. It was a lifesaver. In a nutshell, RPM is a very quick and easy way to take large goals and break them down into daily steps. It covers all areas of your life and is a great tool that will make you look like a god in the eyes of your employees because you it enables you to accomplish a lot with relative ease.

Speaking of employees, the transition phase is when you need to start thinking about being an owner and not a worker in your business. That means offloading your responsibilities to other people, preferably a president, CEO, or COO who can handle the day-to-day running of the business. Because this person will bring a fresh set of eyes into your business, he or she will very quickly realize where the cracks are and can start repairing them. Furthermore, this allows you to take a step back outside of the trenches so that you can look at the bigger picture of the business, such as financing and corporate strategy. But be warned: This phase can cause as much anxiety to an entrepreneur as the launch phase. It's very difficult for most people to let go of their baby, even if they are now grown adults. Similarly, you will experience stress, and you will need to force yourself to back away and let people do their job. It will probably be one of the toughest things you will ever do. I certainly know that is true for me.

CHAPTER 11

Exit Strategies

When you are meeting with investors, the first thing they will ask is, "What is your exit strategy?" This is because they want to know how they will exit their investment. So it is worth your time to contemplate how you will exit or indeed monetize your investment. You need to come to the realization that you will not be running this business forever. That used to be the norm in business, but not anymore. Markets shift too fast, and your children might not have the same passions you have and thus will show no interest in running the "family business" when you're ready to retire. So it's best to plan ahead right from the beginning.

If you are planning on raising money, you need an exit strategy, period. It needs to be concise and well thought out in advance so that you don't stumble into a trap, or worse, so that you don't provide an easy excuse for an investor to pass on your investment opportunity.

IPO vs. Strategic Sale

There comes a point when you will want to cash in on your hard work. This is particularly true when you start noticing that you no longer have the passion for your work that you once had. Perhaps the day-to-day aspects of running your business are boring you, or you are established enough in your business that now you want to diversify your risk, take out some money, and put it into a safe haven or another industry. Perhaps you just want that million-dollar mansion or that vacation home in the Bahamas.

There are two ways of cashing in: by making a strategic sale to another company or by taking your company public. The two routes are both painstaking and need to be timed accordingly, but they do feature different parameters that should be considered beforehand.

Going Public

For many years I thought going public was the ultimate achievement. It was at the top of my list of goals to achieve. I thought that when I pressed the button to open the stock exchange there would be fireworks, a string quartet, and a new private jet in my garage. But frankly speaking, the experience was rather anti-climactic, leaving me with the question, "Is this it?"

Sure, my net worth shot up by tens of millions on the first day of trading, but it also went back down millions when the market collapsed during the 2008 credit crisis. Given the newly added headache of dealing with the financial authorities, a board of directors, hostile shareholders, and the market in general, I would think twice in the future before taking a company public. The challenges that come with it are not for the fainthearted. They can also massively distract you from the things you need to get done.

The biggest challenge in taking a company from private to public is the major shift in priorities that decision brings. As a private company, you have the benefit of taking a long-term strategic approach, whereas in a public company, you will constantly be under pressure to meet your quarterly numbers. The second big shift is that there are now more people meddling in the affairs of your business, including a board of directors, analysts, and the arena of public opinion. It's a tough change for any entrepreneur. I don't care how big or how small you are, going public is a nerve-wracking experience for any company founder.

Strategic Sale

My CEO found a California company that was interested in acquiring my business. When you are selling a company, you have to think a bit beyond the dollar amount you're going to earn from the sale. You also need to consider the fact that you, as the largest single owner of the company, will most likely have to work with the new owner for the next two to three years after you complete the sale. This is how the buyer ensures a proper transition from you, the previous owner. Therefore, it is imperative that you like the people who are buying your company. As always, the price has to be right.

When you're selling a public company, you have to remember that you will be locked up. That is, you will be paid after all other shareholders. A portion of your cash payment might also be what's called an earn-out. That simply means that some of the money you're being paid may be dependent on some future milestones, after the company has sold, that you will be directly responsible for achieving. Try to avoid them at all cost – even if it means a little less money up front. The new owners may not fund the business as you have in the past, making it impossible for you to reach those milestones. The process can be very lengthy and expensive, and it can take several months to get even close to a sales agreement. Very often, you will be forced to wear multiple hats because not only are you acting for yourself, but on behalf of your shareholders too. Nonetheless, sometimes it is better to sell the company than to maintain ownership of it, particularly if your largest shareholder wants to get out. On other occasions, it might be important for you to retain ownership in the company. Finally, be aware that a new owner might take your company in a new direction that might not necessarily be in agreement with your initial goals for your company.

Losing It All and Starting Anew

One of the greatest skills that any entrepreneur can have is knowing when to throw in the towel. Many new business owners ignore the inevitable until it's too late, or they are so underwater that they will never be able to recover. The most successful business owners know when to shut a business. Richard Branson is a great example. His management team is ruthless in this area. For all the two hundred or so Virgin businesses that exist, there is a slew of failed ones including Virgin Car, Virgin Express, Virgin Cola, Virgin Bike, and Virgin Charters, just to name a few. In fact, they have a system of milestones that a company must achieve in the first year of operation, and if it doesn't, it's slated for decommissioning. How's that for being ruthless? I have had to make the same decision with some of my companies.

The first business I started was a consulting business. It was a bust. I shuttered it. Over the years I had a couple of businesses that I started working on and closed within twelve months before ever actually launching them to the public, including an online casino, a hotel company, and a private jet charter company to name a few. I was lucky that I identified fatal flaws well before actually launching those businesses. I love those industries, in particular the aviation sector, but I couldn't find a way to make money at a 3 percent gross margin. As much as I love the industry, I walked away because I have financial discipline.

The real reason for being ruthless is to limit losses. If you spent $50,000 on launching a new business and it is not succeeding, why would you spend another $150,000 by mortgaging your house and then going bust anyway? You wouldn't believe how many people make that mistake. It's insanity. It is not logical. But it happens because people can't remove themselves from their emotional connection to the business. It's OK to have a failed business, though, as long as you learn a lesson from the failure. A Harvard education is much more expensive. See it as a tuition fee of life.

So make sure that right from the beginning you have a set of defined goals and milestones that are realistic, tangible, and measurable. Positive EBIDTA (Earnings Before Interest Depreciation, Taxes, and Amortization) or positive cash flow are the only two good indicators. If a business is not meeting your EBIDTA or cash flow goals, find a fast solution to the problem, and if you can't fix it within six months, shut it down. Be ruthless. It's better to walk away and start something different. Your time is better served focusing on a business that is successful and will grow and make you lots of money, rather than trying to keep a miserable business afloat that will disenchant you and not grow your wealth.

CHAPTER 12

Keeping Your Sanity

Forced Vacations and Why You Need Them

Most of the people I talk to are amazed at the fact that I force my employees to go on vacation a minimum of six weeks per year. The American work ethic doesn't jive with my understanding of what it takes for someone to operate at maximum efficiency. The industry that I work in is very stressful. We deal with a lot of bureaucracy and it can be frustrating. Not only do I make sure that my employees go on vacation; I also make sure that I go on vacation.

As an entrepreneur, it can be very difficult for me to get away two or three weeks at a time. So instead, I rely on mini vacations.

Mini vacations are generally a Thursday to Sunday getaway: four days somewhere that is not too far away and not too expensive, but is away from the day-to-day bustle of business where you can give your mind a rest. For me that place used to be Nassau Bahamas. I like it there. I've gone there for many years because it's one of the few places on this planet where I can turn my brain off—and that's the most important part—so that I can take refuge. Don't take the family. Do not take the children. Just go by yourself, on your own, so that you can recover and recoup. I made the mistake of turning Nassau into a place of business by starting a subsidiary down there. Business in the Caribbean is great, but I lost my place of refuge, because now when I am there I am stuck in meetings too. So I had to scour the world for a new place of refuge. Luckily, I found it in the island of St. Barth's, a tiny little island in the French Caribbean that is somewhat difficult to get to. When I go there, I try not to work. If I do, I keep it to fifteen minutes per day. With today's communications, it is very easy to do conference calls, video calls, and email without ever having to see someone in person. So take advantage of this technology and take a break. However, even better is to turn the gadgets off when you are on vacation. The world will not come to an end. And if you have read this book, then you will have hired good people who can handle your absence.

Learn to Delegate

I used to do everything myself. Everything was under my control, and I used to work very long hours, often from 7 a.m. to midnight, every day of the week. I didn't learn until recently the importance of delegating work to others, and I paid for it dearly. I gained about forty pounds, lost my health, and ultimately ended up getting – mononucleosis—a very debilitating sickness that drains you of all your energy.

I have had several conversations with the likes of Richard Branson, Tony Robbins, and other very successful entrepreneurs who run a multitude of companies; one key thing they all said to me was to make sure I found a good management team so that I could concentrate on other more important things. I took those words of wisdom to heart. I hired a CEO, I hired a new CFO, and I hired someone who was very capable on the development side of running a business. This freed up time for my personal life, but it also allowed me to focus on strategy, and finding the direction that my company needed to go in for further business development. I also developed a very lean and flat management structure that allowed people to make decisions and take ownership of the work that they were doing.

I've come full circle, from a person who used to be unwilling to delegate his work, to someone who takes a hands-off approach to his employees, knowing they have good judgment and trusting that they will make the right decisions. Even if they don't, I can still make sure that they learn from their mistakes. That allows them to grow in their jobs and provides them with a challenge. It's surprising how people will thrive in an environment that is both fun and challenging.

Family and Relationships

In my quest for entrepreneurial success, I somewhat sacrificed my personal life, not that I didn't have a great partner who put up with all of my late nights, early meetings, and missed dinners. However, the bigger problem was that I put so much energy into my business that I forgot to take care of myself. That resulted in a separation, ill health, and a lot of money lost. It is imperative for any entrepreneur who takes on the challenge of starting a new business to remember to take care of his or her health, family, and loved ones.

Your Health

Your health is very important; never forget that. In my previous business in the music industry, I was running around every day and evening, and spending the wee late hours in the nightclubs, talking with DJs and very often ending up on the dance floor. But with my new business, I was stuck behind a desk from 9:00 a.m. to midnight almost daily, and I didn't get out anymore. Most of the time when Fridays rolled around, I was too tired to even contemplate going out or meeting up with friends. Couple that with stress (in particular financial stress), and it can very easily interrupt your daily routine and your natural desire to connect with others in social settings.

About two years ago I got a little wakeup call from my father who laid it on me. I also happened to see the documentary *Food, Inc.*, which awakened me to the reality of how badly I was eating and how it was destroying my health.

Being the goal setter I am, I decided to adopt a vegetarian diet. I completely reversed my routine by ending my day at the pool. Within about a month, I had already lost fifteen pounds. Investing in your health is the best investment you can make as an entrepreneur. The biggest asset you will ever have is not the car, the yacht, the mansion, or even that CEO business card. But rather, it is your health, and the ability to live your life to the fullest, to have fun along the way, and to share your wealth with your loved ones. It's not the material things that make it all worthwhile, but the joy we get out of the relationships we maintain, whether those are at our place of work or in our personal life. If you can keep your focus on that single priority—the ultimate experience of joy in human relationships, then it will be easier to get through the entrepreneurial rough patches.

Conclusion

When you're an entrepreneur, your work becomes your life and your life becomes your work. Your approach to the nuances of life differs greatly from that of the nine-to-fivers. In this book, I have attempted to combine a broad range of subjects to give you a complete, realistic idea of what it takes to be an entrepreneur. I believe it is important to realize that being an entrepreneur takes more than incorporating your business and having the mindset of "if I build it, they will come"—meaning, those you hope will be your future customers. It requires a deeper look into your ideas, your management style, and your work-life balance. This is just as important at the beginning of your business as it is later on when you are successful. You have to constantly remind yourself of these nuances to remain on top of the game, because if one falls out of balance, it will very quickly take the others with it. As an entrepreneur, you have to be open to change in all stages of your personal life, your work, and your business. You also have to be able to admit failure when it is warranted. There is a reason why overnight successes are always ten years in the making. Failing at something is not a failure as long as you learn a lesson and become better the next time around. So, above all else, never let them tell you it cannot be done. Never let them see you down, and absolutely never give up on your dream. It is that unwillingness to give up when the chips are down, that defines entrepreneurs and legacies are created.

www.ingramcontent.com/pod-product-compliance
Lightning Source LLC
Chambersburg PA
CBHW062113040426
42337CB00042B/2044